THE
NUTCRACKER CHRONICLES

"Smart, vivid, and full of heart, Kovac nails what it feels like to be a little kid with a big dream, then fearlessly leads us to that dream's realization and—maybe best of all—to what comes after."

—SARA NOVIĆ,
New York Times bestselling author of *True Biz* and *Girl at War*

"This book dazzles with vulnerability and vibrates with the unbridled innocence and energy of youthful convictions, reminding us that certain human needs, like love and confidence and simply being seen, are inside jobs, and while the human body has its limits, the search for that single thing that makes our hearts soar is illimitable. This book is a triumph for our times and a tribute to every one of us who knows what it means to feel more than see the beauty around and in us."

—PUTSATA REANG,
author of Pacific Northwest Book Award winner *Ma and Me*

"A voice as distinctive and moving as they come. Kovac writes from deeply inside the experience and through it all we are privy to what isn't seen on stage, for she not only knows she tells, 'exactly what's happening on the other side of the curtain.' Janine Kovac has penned a new ballet of prose that will stay with you long after that final curtain call."

—TONI MIROSEVICH, author of *Spell Heaven*

"Filled with vivid, transporting descriptions of dance, from the fabric of sumptuous costumes to the fascinating mechanics of balance, *The Nutcracker Chronicles* is a true insider's take on what transpires behind the scenes, on and off stage, and in the hearts and bodies of dancers. Kovac highlights not just the pure beauty of ballet, but the interconnected waves of enthrallment, hard work, setbacks, celebration, and self-possession that shaped her life from childhood lessons to professional fruition and success."

—SAVALA NOLAN, author of *Don't Let It Get You Down: Essays on Race, Gender, and the Body*

"Janine Kovac's evocative memoir of her life in dance, punctuated by all the *Nutcrackers* in her long and circuitous career, takes us on a journey that is both relatable and extraordinary. Her precise memory for poignant detail took me straight back to those early days of our shared Ballet El Paso *Nutcrackers*! Brava Janine, you so expertly portray all the complicated facets of a life devoted to dance and all the shapes that life can take."

—TANYA RIVERO WARREN, ABC News anchor and former New York City Ballet dancer

Janine Kovac's witty, honest, heartfelt ballet-centric memoir moves with the grace of dance, from little girl enthusiasms, oven-baked toe shoes, petty jealousies, and nasty teachers to the tireless competition of international auditioning, performance and struggling to make a life on stage. For those who love dance, for those who know nothing of dance, this bittersweet book will speak to you about perseverance, friendship, and what is really important.

—LAUREN KESSLER, author of *Raising the Barre: Big Dream, False Starts and My Midlife Quest to Dance the Nutcracker*

Janine Kovac's vividly written and cleverly structured memoir will give anyone delighted with 'Nutcracker' an insider understanding of what it's like to be a working dancer, as well as deepen their understanding of the Tchaikovsky classic.

—RACHEL HOWARD, dance critic for the *San Francisco Chronicle* and author of *The Risk of Us*

THE
NUTCRACKER
CHRONICLES

THE
NUTCRACKER
CHRONICLES

A

Fairytale Memoir

JANINE KOVAC

SHE WRITES PRESS

Published 2024
Printed in the United States of America
Print ISBN: 978-1-64742-792-4
E-ISBN: 978-1-64742-793-1
Library of Congress Control Number: 2024913239

For information, address:
She Writes Press
1569 Solano Ave #546
Berkeley, CA 94707

Interior design by Stacey Aaronson

She Writes Press is a division of SparkPoint Studio, LLC.

Names and identifying characteristics have been changed to protect the privacy of certain individuals.

For the Bunheads of Ballet El Paso

ACT I

OVERTURE

YOU START OUT IN THE AUDIENCE. WE ALL DO. YOU WEAR your frilliest dress or the one that gets the most air when you twirl. Your hair is perfect, and your face is shiny. You glow from the inside out.

You clutch your ticket or your program, whichever you have been allowed to hold, and move at a snail's pace toward tonight's seats. The lobby bursts with patrons: blue-haired ladies with canes, slick-looking gentlemen, and little girls who look just like you. There's a bottleneck at the entrance to the house. The black pantsuit at the door examines each ticket, as if there might be a winning lottery number on it, and then directs you to the left or to the right.

You find your row and you find your seat and you sit on the edge of it, not because you are too excited to sit all the way back but because you are too small. You are like Lewis Carroll's shrunken Alice in those plush red-velvet seats.

The chatter of the people in the rows around you is a dull roar, and you can hear the orchestra warming up above the din. More black pantsuits down there, more important ones. If your seat is close enough, maybe your mother will let you walk—don't run!—to the orchestra pit to see the musicians practice bits and pieces. There's always the trumpet from the Spanish variation playing the first eight bars over and over. The harpist practices her waterfall of notes from "Waltz of the Flowers," and the celesta skitters through the last *ménage* of the Sugar Plum's solo.

Years later, you are the mother whispering, "Don't run!" as your daughter scampers toward the orchestra pit. No one here knows that you, too, were once a ballet dancer in this very opera house.

You danced as a determined warrior mouse, a snowflake shimmering in the lightest possible shade of blue, a flower waltzing in pastels of layered tulle, and in the final years before retirement, a candy soloist in the Land of the Sweets.

You know exactly what's happening on the other side of the curtain. The stage has shrunk because the party scene furniture takes up half the square footage. The Spanish girls dance with the trumpet's opening bars, but he never plays the part they actually need to rehearse. In the dressing rooms, dancers are sewing shoes and applying finishing touches of makeup to their faces, carrying out their superstitious rituals. They are in various stages of stretching and smoking and praying.

Please let these shoes/this costume/my ankle last one more show.

Some of those dancers you will see tonight will be better than you were. Some of them not as good. But all of them are younger and healthier. They will be onstage, and you will be sitting here reliving each piqué arabesque, every grand jeté. Your legs will twitch. Your heart will flutter. Your body will remember all of the criticisms but none of the blisters. An old lament will resurface and echo like a motif from the battle scene.

If only I'd had more time.

At 8:03 p.m., the stage manager clears the area with a heavy whisper and a wave of his hand. The dancers scurry off into the wings and back to their dressing rooms. The soloist who thinks the rules don't apply to him flitters off one more series of turns.

Meanwhile, it is twilight in the theater, the brief stretch of time between waking and dreaming. The lights are lowered. The last of the cherry cough drops are dispensed to stave off dry throats. In the pit, the musicians tune their instruments, swelling and swaying until they converge as one. The conductor raises his baton. The orchestra waits for its cue.

Just like that, it is Christmas Eve onstage.

Your daughter's eyes are wide, sparkling with excitement and anticipation. You know exactly what she is thinking.

If only I could be one of them.

WAITING IN THE WINGS

1978

WHEN I WAS SEVEN, MY AMBITIONS WERE STRAIGHTFORWARD: I wanted to be a psychologist in the Army, like my dad, and I wanted to be a ballerina, like the plastic figure that twirled around on the top of my music box.

Truthfully, the ballerina looked nothing like a dancer and not just because her legs were fused together. She had a tutu made from plastic netting, and her gold pointe shoes were really just a glob of paint. She was fake and flimsy and offered no clues as to what a real ballerina might do. I had to use my imagination.

Sometimes, when my mother was busy with my little brothers, I'd shut the door to my bedroom and change into a slip that was supposed to be worn under Sunday school dresses. It was pale yellow with lace along the hem and a tiny rose sewn into the neckline. It didn't look like underwear like my other slips. It didn't look like a tutu either, but when I'd twirl fast enough, the skirt would catch the air, and I'd imagine sparkles coming out of my skin and filling up the whole world.

My ballet lessons were held at Fort Bliss, the army base where my dad was stationed, which sat at the foot of the Franklin Mountains in El Paso, Texas. Not far from the army hospital where my brother had been born, next to the commissary where my mother shopped, and across from the big building where my father talked to other army guys in green fatigues and crisp tans, there was a big room for kids. On one side there was a carpet and a wooden boat full of toys. On the other, a linoleum floor, a record player, and a ballet teacher named Kathy. I spent a year's worth of Thursday afternoons dancing orderly patterns of steps. Then, two months into fourth grade, Kathy suggested to my mother that I switch to a teacher who had more advanced students.

"Renée is a dancer with Ballet El Paso, just like me," Kathy said. "Why don't you come watch us dance in *The Nutcracker*, and you can decide if you want to take lessons from her."

I had been to a ballet performance once before. I knew the stage was like a magic box suspended in space, and every time the curtains opened, it had new furniture. I could tell the back wall wasn't a real wall; it was just a sheet with scenery painted on it. It was as if the dancers were jumping around in a cartoon.

Kathy danced lots of parts in *The Nutcracker*. She was a snowflake, a flower, Spanish Chocolate, and something called a "mirliton" of unidentifiable origin. She was listed so many times in the program I thought Kathy might be the star of *The Nutcracker*. But she wasn't. The star was Clara.

Clara was not danced by a little girl but by a short grown-up named Renée Segapeli, who, I discovered when matching names in the program to the headshots of the company members, was actually the prima ballerina for Ballet El Paso. She was also the ballet teacher Kathy had recommended to my mother. Some years Renée danced the part of Clara and some years she danced the part of the Sugar Plum Fairy. The year I went to take classes in her studio just across the railroad tracks from Juárez, she danced both.

For the first part of the ballet, the stage looked like an old-fashioned living room, complete with a fancy red-velvet love seat.

The Christmas tree was obviously just painted on a huge tree-shaped cloth. But unlike the music-box stage of my plastic ballerina, it looked like there might be real magic in that fake scenery.

I watched as Clara's bratty brother Fritz pranced around. I knew he was a troublemaker—I'd read the synopsis in the program. But even if I hadn't, it was clear from the way he jutted out his chin and poked Clara with his sword when no one was looking. Fritz was also danced by a grown-up (who also danced as the Mouse King, Kathy's partner in Spanish, and as one of the Russian dancers). When he broke Clara's nutcracker, I was so mad I thought I was going to cry.

Fritz, on the other hand, looked terribly pleased with himself. He even had the nerve to taunt Clara with a little jig. His teasing was short-lived, however, because one of the cousins snitched on him. Discipline was delivered swiftly. I was not the only one who cheered at this.

In the second act, giant lollipops and candy canes replaced the painted sheet of living-room walls. Clara, now the Sugar Plum Fairy, had changed into a pink tutu, and the rest of the dancers—Chocolate from Spain, Coffee from Arabia, Tea from China, plus a few flowers with green bodices and petaled gowns—bowed to her. She shone with a special glow that the other dancers didn't quite have.

She was like a ball of light, as if she knew a special secret. Maybe if I followed her around, I could learn how to be a ball of light too.

At the end of the ballet, Renée/Clara/Sugar Plum and her Nut-cracker Prince stepped into a boat painted like a walnut. Even though I could see the wire that lifted them up across the stage, it was as if they were really flying. Stage magic. The conductor waved his hands up and down, signaling music that crashed like cymbals climbing stairs. On the final note, the curtain closed. When it opened again, rows of dancers ran back onstage. They stood there waiting while we clapped for them. Renée and her prince were the last to come onstage. They ran in front of the other dancers straight to the middle. Everyone clapped loudest for them. Then Renée ran offstage and came back holding the hand of a man in a black pantsuit and guided him to the front. I knew he was the conductor. He didn't seem to have done as much as the dancers had, and he certainly didn't look like a ball of light, but we cheered for him anyway.

Just when I thought it was time to stop clapping, a woman in clunky heels handed Renée the biggest bouquet of flowers I'd ever seen. Renée took a single rose and handed it to the Nutcracker Prince. He bowed to her, and the applause started all over again. My hands stung from slapping them together for so long. My head buzzed and my chest felt fluttery, like the best kind of dizzy.

Like salmon swimming upstream, my mother and I worked our way to the mustard-yellow door that divided the audience from the dancers. Kathy was waiting for us. She was still wearing her brown tutu from the Spanish variation.

"Janine, this is Renée Segapeli," she said.

Face-to-face with a real sugar plum fairy, I almost choked on my disappointment. Her face was caked with makeup that looked more orange than pink, and her chest was dotted with sweat. She wore huge fake eyelashes, and if that didn't make her eyes look garish enough, she also had big black lines drawn over her eyebrows, white paint on her brow bones, and a tiny red dot on the inside corner of each eye. She had brown streaks on either side of her nose and along her chin. She wore a fancy silk bathrobe draped over her tutu the way a duck might wear a dress. On her feet she wore fuzzy slippers.

I must have looked scared because Renée laughed and took my hand.

"Have you ever been backstage before?" She led me to the wings, and my heart sank. I thought that going backstage meant I'd get to sit in the clouds around the magic box, but it was just a huge warehouse of a room with brick walls. It was worse than fake; it was as if I'd been tricked.

On the sides of the stage there were tables, and I recognized things dancers had held and masks they had worn. Everything was clearly labeled with masking tape. NUTCRACKER read one strip of tape, as if it needed a name tag to identify it. DO NOT TOUCH read another sign.

Closer to the stage, flanked by long velvet curtains, black poles with boxes of tissue taped to their stems held fat lights that faced the stage. Along the walls, thick ropes hung from the ceiling to the floor. It reminded me of the piano strings in my mother's upright at home. If I were a mouse stuck inside a Steinway, it might feel like this.

The dancer who had performed the role of Fritz, the Mouse King, Spanish, and Russian strutted out of his dressing room. He was not wearing makeup. He wore jeans and sunglasses. And he was smoking a cigarette. He gave the Sugar Plum Fairy a kiss on the cheek, and she kissed him back, leaving lipstick on his face. They were friends. I could tell.

Something clicked in my brain.

As much as I wanted to believe it was real, I knew it wasn't possible for boxes to float in the clouds in the middle of El Paso, Texas. But the fluttery feeling in my chest had been real. Renée's ball of light—that was real too. All these things—ropes, lights, painted sheets, and dancers who glowed onstage—created an illusion that made people feel as giddy as if they had actually gone to a fairy-tale land full of sweets.

Maybe if I danced on that stage, I could climb back into the belief that magic was real life. Maybe I could turn the brick walls back into clouds.

I liked this idea very much.

Renée's ballet studio was on the top floor of an old brewery on a street so small my mother couldn't find it on the map. There were no signs anywhere. There wasn't even a parking lot—just a lot of gravel and a big dumpster. The building—such a faint yellow it almost looked pink, and such a pale pink it looked like the sky just after dawn—was visible from the freeway. We saw it clearly each time my mother missed the exit. And if my mother missed the exit, we'd find ourselves in Mexico instead of ballet class. By the time we'd make it back over the border, class would be over.

The lift to the top was a freight elevator, the kind that required pulling on a strap to close the double set of heavy doors before it jolted to life and chugged up the three stories to Renée's studio. It was faster to take the stairs.

At the top, there was a small waiting room for mothers and little brothers. Renée and her boyfriend, who was a DJ for the local rock station, lived in back of the studio. Their cat roamed freely between the ballet studio and the back rooms, and when she had kittens, they did too.

An arched doorway led to a dance space with a cement floor painted a shiny dark red and cathedral windows that overlooked downtown El Paso and the *mercados* of Juárez. I thought it looked just like the studios in New York that I'd seen in my issues of *Dance Magazine.* I was too short to see out the windows when I stood facing the barre until I rose to demi pointe. Then I could see the Franklin Mountains in the distance, the interstate in the foreground. The longer I balanced, the more I could see.

Renée always wore bright scarves, layers of plastic pants, and tattered leg warmers. Duct tape held her leather flat shoes intact, just like Natalia Makarova, the ballerina who'd recently defected from Russia. Or maybe it was Natalia Makarova who tried to look like Renée Segapeli.

I had my own fashion statement: leotards with matching tights, with a different color for each day of the week. On Mondays I wore pink. Tuesdays I wore light blue. Wednesdays were black, Thursdays red, and Fridays purple.

Thursdays were the best thing about dancing at Renée's studio because that was the day I had private lessons. I basked in Renée's special light, in much the same way the kitten she'd given me stretched out on my bed to soak up the sunshine that streamed in from the window. On Thursdays, the attention was all mine.

In my ballet classes at Fort Bliss, I knew Kathy's eyes were on me and that the other students copied me. It happened with a regularity that made it feel inevitable, the same way I knew I'd spelled all the words right on my weekly spelling tests. We did the same combinations to the same music, always in the same order. I loved this almost as much as I loved pulling the focus of everyone's attention. The preordained combinations were like a designated flight pattern.

At Renée's ballet studio, things were different. Everyone else was older and taller, and some of them even drove cars. They knew steps I hadn't learned yet, and because every class brought new combinations and patterns, I often felt like a little kid who gets to sit at the grown-ups' table but can't join in the conversation. But I learned something: I didn't have to be the best dancer to pull the teacher's eye. I just had to be myself.

One day a visitor came to class. His name was David, and he was the same dancer who'd performed the role of Fritz.

"Isn't she remarkable?" Renée said to him. "I show the combination front and to the right, and she'll do it to the back and to the left. Every time. She doesn't even know she's reversing it!"

I wasn't sure what she meant, but I did know Renée thought I was remarkable. That's all that mattered.

And then one Thursday: catastrophe.

It started out like any other Thursday. I ran up the stairs on the verge of being late, while my mother and little brothers took their chances in the creaky freight elevator. As I stripped down to my red leotard and matching red tights, I heard voices from inside the studio. Sometimes the DJ boyfriend hung out with his friends in one of the back rooms during class, but these were female voices.

I hurried into the studio to take my special place at the barre only to find someone was already standing in it.

It was a little girl. She was shorter than I was, and she was cuter than I was. From the way she was warming up with her leg on the barre, I could see she was also more flexible than I was.

"Janine!" Renée gave me a warm smile as she took my hand. "I want you to meet someone. This is Dee Bee." She motioned to the little girl, who grinned brightly. I tried not to glower. I might not have tried that hard.

"Dee Bee is in the fifth grade too. She's going to start taking lessons here. Isn't that great? Now you won't be all alone on Thursdays. And she lives near you! Maybe you can carpool to class."

Dee Bee's mother turned to me and smiled. She was also short and cute, and I hated both of them.

"Let's take our places at the barre!" Renée tucked a wisp of hair under her scarf and began to demonstrate a plié combination. Dee Bee's mother gave a little wave and retreated to the waiting room to exchange phone numbers with my mother.

Dee Bee immediately assumed a perfect first position. Tummy in. Chin up. She was still standing in my place and Renée had not asked her to move, so I stood behind them, turning my toes out to the side more than I ever had before, sucking in my stomach to the point of holding my breath.

"Very nice!" Renée purred. "Now let's begin. Demi plié and straighten. Repeat. Chin up! Shoulders down! Like a drop of water could fall from your shoulder down your fingertip."

My first inclination had been right. Dee Bee was better than I was. Her feet were more arched. Her back was more arched. She could balance longer, turn more, jump higher, and she never went to the back and to the left when Renée demonstrated a combination to the front and to the right. My only solace was that I was still younger, if only by three months.

Things got worse. *Nutcracker* rehearsals started, and sometimes, after class, Renée would drive Dee Bee to their rehearsal in her dusty-pink Karmann Ghia while I went home with my mother and little brothers. Dee Bee, I discovered from eavesdropping, had been chosen to dance the part of the Bunny in the battle scene. Not *a* bunny. *The* Bunny. Now I knew I hated her.

Then . . . a lucky break. Ballet El Paso needed six pages for *Sleeping Beauty*, and both Dee Bee and I had been chosen to dance. Now I was the one behind the mustard-yellow door dancing in the magic box in the clouds.

AT THE PARTY

THE FIRST TIME I MET THE DIRECTOR OF BALLET EL PASO IN PERSON, I thought she might be a witch. Ingeborg Heuser didn't look anything like her glamorous full-page portrait in the ballet programs, in which she'd posed for the camera on a fancy couch. Dressed in a full-length gown of linen and white lace, her hair was coiffed to perfection on top of her head like spun sugar. She had laughter in her eyes and a smile on her face that made her teeth look even. In her photograph, she radiated like a Prussian countess.

But in person, her green eyes were wild, as if she could read your thoughts. Her red hair was more of a bird's nest than a hairstyle, and her skin was like the leather of a cowboy saddle. She claimed she kept it smooth with a cream from crushed pearls she kept refrigerated for nightly application to her face and neck. She had the slow, lumbering gestures of a dinosaur mixed with the temperament of Joan Collins from *Dynasty*.

She was not clumsy but definitely nothing like the lithe, graceful Renée. It was difficult to imagine she had been a soloist with the Deutsche Oper Berlin during World War II before fleeing to Italy to be a movie star. Rumor had it that she came to America when she married a US serviceman from Fort Bliss, and when she was a teenager, she had danced for Hitler.

In one retelling, she slipped and fell at Hitler's feet when he came to watch her dance. She could barely contain her tears at the humiliation of it, and when an SS officer knocked at her dressing room door, the other girls were sure she was in trouble. Instead, she was handed a box of chocolates—a rare wartime commodity—and a note from der Führer himself. He admired her courage, he wrote. She was an excellent example of "German female quality."

Later, when my own ballet career took me to Germany and Italy, I would hear other stories.

"She was so bowlegged they called her 'piano legs,'" one of my ballet masters told me. "You could hit a croquet ball between those knees."

Whatever her true origins, Ms. Heuser put Ballet El Paso on the map. During her tenure at the University of Texas at El Paso, her dancers secured contracts with companies such as San Francisco Ballet, Boston Ballet, the Royal Ballet of Denmark, and even New York City Ballet. She was able to woo guest artists from American Ballet Theatre, Mexico City, and the Royal Ballet of London.

Ballet El Paso was located within the fine arts department of the university's campus. There were two ballet studios plus an auditorium with dressing rooms, a sewing room, a costume room, and even a wing for building scenery. Years later when I danced abroad, I realized that this was a European convention. Ballet companies trained and rehearsed in the same buildings in which they performed.

Ms. Heuser's position as a professor and department chair gave her access to resources that allowed Ballet El Paso to flourish. Renée said Ms. Heuser had installed a real sprung Marley floor—the kind they had in Germany. Even New York didn't have floors like this, she had said.

✳

Unlike Renée, Ms. Heuser played favorites and her favoritism had no formula. Sometimes she fawned over dancers because they were new or came from a bigger city. Other times she showed preference for the dancers who'd been with her the longest. Sometimes she seemed mean, like when she barked at Kendal, who'd wanted to understudy Snow Queen. Other times she acted warm and motherly, like when she purred her praise for Kendal's weight loss. No one seemed to stay in her good graces for long, though.

On the day of my first ballet class with Ms. Heuser, my mother drove me to Ballet El Paso's studios at the fine arts building. Grown-ups called it UTEP. To me it was the place where the real ballet dancers were.

Mirrors lined the front of the studio. Laminated ballet posters from Deutsche Oper Berlin and Hamburg Ballett hung on the studio's brown cinder block walls. I didn't need to read German to understand they were pictures of famous ballerinas: Eva Evdokimiva in *Les Sylphides* and Gigi Hyatt in *Manon*. Underneath barres bolted onto thick planks of wood were globs of gum in every possible color—even fluorescent yellow. Floor-to-ceiling windows gave the nosier parents a glimpse of goings-on from the outside. I was grateful my mother wasn't one of them.

As we waited to be called into the studio, one of the girls pointed to the white bulge under my tights at the base of my leotard.

"What's *that*?" she asked. She didn't introduce herself, but I knew her name was Sofia.

I turned red. "It's my underwear."

"Why do you wear *underwear*?" Sofia made a face and looked

at her friend, who raised her eyebrows. It wasn't a question. It was a statement: *You are a loser because you wear underwear under your tights.*

"You don't wear underwear?" I made a face too. But unlike Sofia, my question was an actual question. This might explain why I was the only person in ballet class whose underwear showed through no matter how often I pulled my leotard down. Was that the solution? No underwear?

Sofia wrinkled her nose. *Only babies wear underwear.* But she didn't say it out loud.

I grimaced back. *That's so gross that you don't wear underwear,* which I didn't say out loud either.

"Your hair isn't in a bun," she continued. "And you're not wearing pink tights."

Because it was a Tuesday, I was wearing my light blue leotard and color-coordinated tights. My hair was secured in two pony-tails pulled up above my ears. I liked the way my hair flipped during pirouettes. It made me feel like I was turning really fast.

"I like to match," I said. "And I like ponytails."

"Well," Sofia scolded, "you need to wear pink tights in ballet class."

Ms. Heuser stood frowning at the front of the studio. Her hair was a dusty orange. When she nodded to us, we entered single file. The other girls took their place at the barre. Even Dee Bee had a place to stand.

"Elephant knees!" Ms. Heuser exclaimed when I entered. Clicking her teeth, she beckoned for me to come to her.

She wasn't saying that my knees were fat; she meant that the wrinkles in the knees of my tights looked like the wrinkles of an elephant. I didn't have a lot of body awareness, but I did know I had bones sticking out in all the right places: knees, elbows, collarbones, and ribs. The problem was that no matter how often I pulled up my tights, after a few knee bends, they were wrinkly again.

Should I curtsy? Stand in fifth position? I was still flipping through possible appropriate reactions when Ms. Heuser stuck her arms down my leotard and pulled me up by my waistband, jerking quickly as if she were stuffing a pillow into a pillowcase. I felt the skin of her forearms on the sides of my chest as she tugged, lifting my feet off the floor.

My new teacher, the Prussian countess, had just given me a wedgie. *One more reason to wear underwear*, I thought. *Protection*.

But it worked. My tights hadn't been pulled up like this . . . well, ever. My knees felt straighter. My back felt straighter. I felt like a dancer.

"When I was a little girl in Germany, tights didn't have elastics. We had to secure them by wrapping a coin in the waistband."

This did not make sense to me, but I was not about to ask for clarification.

"Now let's do your hair. You know, you look just like Liza Minnelli!" Her smile indicated she'd given me a compliment, but I'd seen pictures of Liza Minnelli.

She pulled hairpins out of her pockets and set about pinning each ponytail into a bun. She took her time, completely ignoring the fifteen other students in the class whose hair and tights were already pulled up. I liked being singled out, but I wasn't sure if this was good personal attention or bad.

When she finished pinning my hair, she dismissed me with a curt nod, then turned to the record player and set the needle on the first track. I scrambled to find a place at the barre. The good spots had been taken.

The ballet class shouldn't have been hard. I had done most of the steps in Renée's classes, and even some of the combinations were the same. But it was difficult to understand her instructions and not just because of her accent.

"Boobs in the soup!" she sang to the class during rond de jambe en l'air.

It was a reference to the position of one's torso to a leg extended to the side. The raised leg was supposed to make a circle, stirring boob soup, I supposed. Our bodies were to be angled as if we were providing the main ingredient from our own chests. For a class of sixth graders, we had little to offer, but everyone seemed to manage except for me.

In the center, despite my best efforts, I galloped to the left while the rest of the class chasséd to the right.

Ms. Heuser shook her head. "Why can't you just dance like a pretty girl?" she sighed.

Ingeborg Heuser's insults were like poisonous darts. She called her dancers "cows on ice skates" or suggested they become flight attendants. She compared arched feet to claws, thighs to raw dough. She'd lift the chin of a young student and coo, "I have so many flowers in my garden. You are the weed." She knew just what buttons to push.

But there were rare moments of tenderness. In the spring, we went to her house for a tea party in her garden. Ms. Heuser lived at the foot of the Franklin Mountains in the part of town where the streets were taken from Greek mythology: Olympic, Atlas, Hercules.

Gigi, the live-in maid from Juárez, greeted us at the door. Dee Bee brought flowers. I hadn't thought of that.

The house had white plush carpet, and we had to take our shoes off upon entering. In the parlor stood a china cabinet with claw feet opposite the red-velvet chaise lounge we used in the party scene of *The Nutcracker*. I couldn't see the kitchen, but I knew somewhere in there was a freezer with the face cream made from crushed pearls.

Ms. Heuser wore a white linen pantsuit, the kind that would definitely wrinkle if not hung properly. Gigi wore a black one, and it looked as if it might have come from Ms. Heuser's closet. They had matching hairstyles too, perfectly puffed up around their heads. The only difference was that Ms. Heuser's hair was dyed candy-apple red, while Gigi's was jet-black. I wondered if maybe Ms. Heuser had done her maid's hair, securing it with hairspray and bobby pins the same way she secured wigs for the party scene in *The Nutcracker*. Why not? A tea party was kind of like a performance.

As I walked through the house to the back patio, my bare feet sank into the carpet. Sofia and I sat on the edge of our seats with our china teacup and its matching saucer, ankles crossed, pretending this was normal. I wasn't the only one who'd never been to a tea party before.

In the fall, there were whispers Ms. Heuser had decided the party children in *The Nutcracker* should be real children. Not short grown-ups. Not teenagers.

My mother always said Ballet El Paso's party scene was the best party scene she'd ever seen. Better than the Baryshnikov version on PBS and Pacific Northwest Ballet's movie put together. Better even than San Francisco Ballet.

"When you're watching San Francisco Ballet, you know it's going to be perfect. But with Ballet El Paso, you never knew what was going to happen. It was like a real party."

It was true. Someone's costume might tear, or a piece of precariously built scenery would break. In 1982, the guy who danced the role of Clara and Fritz's father packed his pipe with pot and smoked it onstage; the same guy spiked the party punch with vodka. Once, Drosselmeier didn't show up to the party at all, rumored to be stuck in the drunk tank of a Juárez jail cell. Fritz had to be the one to give Clara the nutcracker, only to grab it from her thirty-two counts later to break it.

At the audition, Dee Bee and I stood along with the other young dancers from Ballet El Paso's feeder schools, while Renée's friend David, the former Fritz and current children's ballet master, lined us up by height at the back of the studio.

Ms. Heuser murmured to David and he nodded. With crisp efficiency, he strode to the center of the room and divided ten girls into three groups: Clara and three girl cousins, Fritz with three boy cousins, and two understudies. Dee Bee and I stood on opposite sides of the room, already experienced enough to wear our best poker faces. If she was excited, she didn't show it. I hoped that I was just as successful at hiding my disappointment.

The news made the papers: Deborah Lampman would be the youngest Clara since Renée Segapeli had first danced the role twenty years earlier. There was no mention of me, the even-younger dancer who was cast as the mischievous brother, or of Sofia, who, at eleven and three-quarters, was the youngest of all of us. Sofia had a special part too. She was the cousin known as The Snitch.

Up until this point, if there was something beyond my capabilities, all I had to do was try harder, like my new skill of completing the Rubik's Cube, which I acquired by reading a book and committing the solutions to memory. But this was different. Trying harder didn't always turn two pirouettes into three. And even when I did manage to add height to my arabesque, Dee Bee's extensions looked more effortless.

Honestly, on a day-to-day basis, Dee Bee wasn't all that bad. She was creative and funny and always making interesting projects. Once she crocheted a bikini out of variegated yarn. Another time she painted a pillowcase and wore it as a shirt. Kids were constantly copying her fashion choices. Plus, she always had watermelon-flavored Hubba Bubba gum that she generously shared with me. She was also really good at passing notes in school because she looked like the kind of student who would never break the rules.

Our first rehearsal for the party scene was scheduled on a Sunday morning. This was a problem.

We were not the kind of family that missed church, especially for something as frivolous as ballet. But my mother knew if I missed rehearsal, I would not get to dance, and that the next time I would not be cast for anything. Reluctantly, she made arrangements with Dee Bee's mother.

Dee Bee's mom drove us in her little orange Opal. It looked like a Corvette. Dee Bee sat in the front seat, braiding a pot holder out of macramé cord. I sat in the back reading a book about Maria Tallchief, one of the first prima ballerinas for New York City Ballet. Maria Tallchief was brown, like me. It seemed as if George Balanchine, her director and husband, was just as hard on his star ballerina as Ms. Heuser was on us.

On Sunday mornings, the Fox Fine Arts building was deserted and dark. Ms. Heuser was always late for classes and rehearsals, so it was a relief to see David marching up the big ramp from the parking lot to unlock the doors to the studio. If David was in charge, not only would we start on time, we'd end on time too.

He began at the beginning: Clara and Fritz take turns looking through a keyhole, trying to see the Christmas tree their parents are decorating in the living room. One by one, their cousins join them.

Of course, in this bare studio with dark brown cinder block walls and floor-to-ceiling mirrors, there was no tree. There were no decorations. No presents. There weren't even any parental party guests. The grown-ups joined rehearsals later.

The steps were easy, and I'd already learned most of them from watching previous years' performances and rehearsals. But it was hard to pretend it was Christmas Eve. It was hard to look at my empty hands and pretend it was a sailboat, or to pretend I was playing a trumpet or beating a drum. I felt silly trying to act. Dee Bee didn't even have a nutcracker for me to break; she and Sofia cradled pointe shoes as their dolls.

"Look excited!" David scolded us. "It's Christmas!" He had exactly six rehearsals to stage the party scene.

During one rehearsal, a tall woman with an expensive handbag stopped by the studio. I knew her as the mother of an understudy for Chef #3. Chefs entered and exited between the Act II divertissements with papier-mâché props fashioned to look like cakes and ice cream sundaes. Even though their part was a walk-on role with minimal choreography, they were still expected to attend every rehearsal.

The woman marched down the hall, slowing her gait as she stepped around the ballet detritus that stood in her way: ashtrays, dance bags, a sewing kit with ribbons and elastic, and the knees and elbows of dancers stretching on the floor, waiting for their rehearsals to start.

"I'm looking for Ingeborg Heuser," she demanded, pronouncing it "How-zer" instead of "Hoyz-sir."

Ms. Heuser stood in her signature black pantsuit. She held her fingers delicately but with purpose, as if her coral-pink nail polish were still wet. Her bright red hair piled on top of her head like cotton candy.

The woman shook her finger. "I'd like to have a word with you. On school nights rehearsals must absolutely end on time!"

Rehearsals always ran late, often ending after ten or eleven o'clock at night. All the parents complained about it, but no one ever confronted Ms. Heuser directly. Not even my mother dared to do such a thing.

Ms. Heuser ignored her.

"César! Come. Help me. I can't find the music for the second act." Ms. Heuser shrugged helplessly. This was part of an impromptu performance. It was her way of saying, "Nobody tells me what to do. I tell other people what to do. See?"

César nodded and quickly stood up, ready for further instructions. The two of them turned their backs to the woman and walked into the studio. César obediently trotted to the music cabinet and rummaged through a series of cassette tapes.

Sofia and I traded sideways glances. I knew we were thinking the same thing: now that girl would never graduate from understudy chef to Chef #3. We turned back to follow David to our rehearsal, leaving the woman alone in the hall with the ashtrays.

✳

On the day Ms. Heuser came to judge our progress in the party scene, we knew our steps perfectly, yet she was displeased.

"What are you doing?" she shrieked. "You are ruining my ballet!" In her breathy accent, somehow more French than German, the words came out "woo-ining." Later Sofia and I would giggle about it, but not on this day.

"You!" She pointed to one of the maids, a young high schooler not advanced enough to dance in "Waltz of the Flowers" and too tall to be a mouse. "You look like a pedestrian! Showing your backside to the audience? You might as well bend over and scratch it." She dropped her arms and mimicked the teenager, making her look like a monkey, not a dancer. It was a cruel imitation and an exaggerated performance. The girl clenched her jaw, determined not to cry.

Ms. Heuser turned to direct her disappointment to one of the older dancers. "And you! Never bring a woman's hand to your lips to kiss it. It means you want to go to bed with her. Always bow down to her hand." She demonstrated with a low bow.

"Dancers! We open in one month. You look like you've never been onstage before!" She threw her hands up in disgust and let them fall to her side. We stood perfectly still.

That was a short tirade. Surely it was not over.

Early in the rehearsal run, someone had chalked a huge Christmas tree on the cinder blocks on the back wall, and from time to time, dancers added to it: ornaments, a window pane, a star on top of the tree. At first it was a way to be festive in this bare studio, but now our cartoon scenery underscored our status as amateurs.

After a heavy sigh, Ms. Heuser walked to the front mirrors. She knew we were looking for a chance to redeem ourselves. She milked the silence. Then she gestured for us to come closer.

"Sit down," she said in a soft voice. "Let me tell you what Christmas was like when I was a little girl."

Dee Bee sat as close as she could, as if to soak up Ms. Heuser's words. I wanted to curry favor too, but spitting distance seemed a little too close. I nudged farther away.

"The first thing you need to know is that in Germany in the winter, it is so dark it is pitch black by three o'clock in the afternoon. The streets are filled with snow. The streetlamps have been lit. It is so cold milk bottles left on the front steps freeze over. No one goes outside unless they have to. If you do go outside—maybe you have been invited to a fancy Christmas party . . ." She looked at our faces, transmitting the message, *I am dropping a hint*.

"If you do go outside, you are wrapped in a scarf and gloves and a hat."

She hunched her shoulders and hugged herself as if attempting to keep warm. Then she blew into her hands and rubbed them together. Her performance was so convincing that Dee Bee, Sofia, and I shivered a bit.

"When I was a little girl, the Christmas Eve party was at my grandmother's house. The children would be locked in a room upstairs. In the dark."

Sofia and I exchanged glances. That explained a lot.

Ms. Heuser snapped off the light. The afternoon sun cast a shadow into the studio. It was just dark enough for her to make her point and just light enough for us to see.

"Even in the dark, you can look out the window and see who is coming to the party next. And if you listen carefully, you can hear the front door open. There, the maid is waiting for the signal to take the coats." She stood tall and rigid, nodding to imaginary help. "Then, you hear footsteps on the staircase. Soon, another cousin will come into the room. You pester them with questions."

Ms. Heuser crouched. She lifted her shoulders, holding the sides of her face in her hands. Looking straight at Dee Bee, she asked, "Did you see the tree?" She paused theatrically. Pulling her hands into fists, she jumped in place. "Were there lots of presents?"

Her eyes shone, and she paused before and after each new tidbit of information, giving us time to process what we heard.

"You are so excited you think you are going to . . ." Another dramatic pause. "Pee!"

Giggles and gasps rippled through the cast. Ms. Heuser had said the word "pee"! It was as if she had cursed.

"And just when you can't stand it any longer, the door opens!"

She held up a finger in warning. "It is the maid, and you know you are not to talk. You walk downstairs on your best behavior. Slowly."

In our version, this was the part where the maids handed out candles and lit them onstage. We had to be careful to hold the candles upright or they would drip wax on the floor.

"First, we sing to the Christ Child."

In a mix of narrative and choreography, this was our entrance into the living room. Slow walks, slow kneel. The orchestra sings with strings and harp, a swirl of magic. Three plucks and then, with the horns of the march, we get to greet our families.

Ms. Heuser stood up and skipped to a couple upstage, two students from the university program good-natured enough to show up on a Sunday for extra credit and tall enough to be parents in the party scene.

"And you say, 'Hello, Auntie. Hello, Uncle. Oh, yes. I've been very good this year.' Make sure you curtsy with a big plié because you know it's rude to just nod your head."

"And you"—she motioned to one college student and mimed putting her hands on the lapels of a jacket—"you say, 'That's a fine cigar.' Or maybe you say, 'I wonder what time it is.'" She mimed taking out a pocket watch. "And then you"—she motioned to the other college student—"you nod and say, 'What a fine watch!'"

She paused to transition from her actor's facade to her teaching one.

"There are two counts for each gesture. The people in the back of the theater need time to see you."

As she made her rounds about the studio, she assumed the identity of each party guest. But it wasn't just her face that changed expressions. She captured an entire personality in her body and gestures. It was in the way she stood, the way she carried her weight. She leaned forward to show eagerness and leaned back to show elegance. After she'd posed as every character, she walked to the front of the studio and sat in her director's chair.

"Now," she said firmly, "let's take it from the top."

Right before winter break, television cameras came to our school to tape a news segment on Dee Bee, Ballet El Paso's youngest performer to ever dance Clara. I stood on the sidelines, waiting patiently for Dee Bee to mention to the interviewer that I played the role of her brother, but she never said a word.

My face stung and my stomach clenched.

"I'm the dancer who plays Fritz!" I wanted to shout. "And I'm three months younger!"

But instead I stood there, watching Dee Bee mug for the cameras. I pushed down the jealousy—a pulsing envy—until it hardened, like a jawbreaker. I'd be so embarrassed if any of the grown-up dancers found out I was jealous. It was a sin.

Nice girls are supposed to be happy for their friends.

✳

For opening night, Dee Bee's hair had been professionally styled with a perfect set of Nellie Oleson curls for her role as Clara. My hair was in curls too, but not the same kind. As Fritz, I wore a wig, and my long hair needed to be coiled up in dozens of pin curls in order for the wig to lie flat.

A volunteer mom had been recruited to pin the soldiers' wigs, but Ms. Heuser insisted on pinning the party children's wigs herself. The counter was littered with boxes of thick pins from Germany and strips of tulle for pulling back stray wisps of hair. On another counter there was a pile of wigs in various conditions. Some looked like cute cabaret wigs, like something Liza Minnelli might wear. Others looked like roadkill.

When Ms. Heuser saw me, she shooed away the dancer in front of her. "Fritz always gets to go first. He needs the best wig."

She smiled and handed me a hairpiece as if it were a prize. Compared to the other wigs on the counter, it was indeed a winner with no matted tufts or weird cowlicks from poor storage. Using both hands on the front of the wig, I held it in place while Ms. Heuser pulled it over my head, and for the next eighty-two seconds, I had her full attention.

Ms. Heuser pinned a wig in the same loving way a decorator might put the finishing touches on a wedding cake, coupled with the speed and efficiency of a NASCAR pit crew. Except instead of piping bags or a socket wrench, she was armed with three-inch hairpins smuggled out of Berlin. Unlike American hairpins, they were longer, thicker, and did not bend. The tips were pointy and sharp, further fueling the rumors that Ms. Heuser had first-person experience with Third Reich weaponry. Each pin had to make its way through fake hair, the netting of the wig, the tulle of the wig band, and a pin curl before a final thrust into the scalp. German engineering delivered every single time.

"If it hurts, you know it won't fall off." She smiled, and our eyes met in the mirror.

Fritz was also the only party child with a real silk tie. I didn't know if the audience could see the difference between silk and the black nylon strips the other boys wore, but up close, the contrast was obvious. The silk was shiny, and when Ms. Heuser tied it in a bow, the loops hung in perfect ovals on the lapels on either side of my blue corduroy jacket.

"I learned how to tie a perfect bow when I first came to this country. I wrapped presents at JCPenney's during the Christmas season."

She beamed at her handiwork, smiling so broadly I felt as if the compliment was for me.

The stage manager calls into the backstage loudspeaker: "Places onstage, please. Places onstage. Let's go, let's go, let's go!"

In the orchestra pit, Mr. Chavez raises his baton.

And just like that, it is Christmas Eve in Germany.

When the curtain opens, Dee Bee and I fight over who gets to look through the keyhole. We don't push too hard; it's more like a stage push. We are cautious, polite.

At first I'm nervous because I'm afraid I'll forget my counts, but then there is a whole list of reasons to be nervous: Sofia's candle spills some wax on the stage when she blows it out. What if someone slips on it? I can't find the maid who is supposed to take my props, and I'm late for handing out presents. I feel like the shy girl at a party, which I would be if I were at a real party.

The stage lights are hot and my wig is itchy, reminding me I have to wear it because I do not dance like a pretty girl.

When Drosselmeier unveils the nutcracker, Dee Bee's eyes light up and her chest expands with a perfect stage gasp, as if she can hardly believe the gift is for her. As if she's never seen a nutcracker before, even though she's spent the last twelve weeks lugging it around and like me, like all of us onstage, probably can't remember a time when she didn't know what a nutcracker looked like.

Faker.

And in that moment, I hate her. I really hate her. I hate that all the teachers at school know she is a little ballerina but none of them even know I dance right beside her in every ballet class and every rehearsal. I hate that the grown-up dancers treat her as something special. I hate her curls that bounce up and down with each piqué arabesque.

But most of all, I hate that stupid nutcracker. It's not a prize. Anyone can see that. The paint is chipped. The boots are scuffed. The head is wobbly from years of use.

The rock in the pit of my stomach shifts. I glower at Clara with her perfect curls in her perfect yellow dress and its perfect bow until she feels my stare.

When she looks up across the stage at me, I wrinkle my nose and make a face. Slowly, like a vapor, the envy makes its way from my stomach to my heart. This is my stage too.

I don't care about Clara's pretty dress or stupid curls. I don't even want that nutcracker. I just don't want her to have it.

When the maid rings the dinner bell and the parents follow her offstage, Dee Bee enters with her precious prop. She tiptoes out, just the way Renée used to do. She looks exactly like a little girl who is excited to have a moment to herself with her new doll.

I'm next. In rehearsal, I walked as if strolling through my

living room. But tonight I think Fritz knows exactly what he's doing; he's trailing his sister. The envy takes its time, like a veil winding itself around my limbs, whispering, "It's okay to be this mad. You are supposed to be envious."

The rest of the cousins enter, and Sofia begs to hold the nutcracker. When Clara hands over the doll, I seize my moment. Grabbing it, I gallop away.

"Nooooooooooooo!" comes a yell from the audience. A little kid. It makes me smile harder. This is my stage. My party.

My music is a set of trills that sounds like a patter of feet running down the stairs, the musical equivalent of a situation getting out of hand. Tonight the trills mirror the unraveling of envy in my belly. Holding the nutcracker over my head, I can feel the audience watching me with a kind of intensity. It feels like a surge, a tidal wave.

I slide into a kneel downstage right and bang the nutcracker on the floor harder than I ever did in rehearsal.

Whack!

The head slides off from the rest of the body. The audience is silent, sucking in a collective breath. I wait two counts, the way Ms. Heuser tells us to. I can feel it again—another message from the audience. They want to see the damage. The cousins onstage are still as statues. They are waiting to react until I give the cue.

I look at Clara and smile.

Oh. I'm sorry. Is this your nutcracker? my eyes say. I hand Clara the headless toy, waiting a beat before I give her the head.

Sofia shakes her finger at me and runs offstage to tattle. I'm in trouble now. Of course, I knew this moment was coming. We've been rehearsing this scene for three months.

It will be an actual spanking, not a stage slap. After years of being spanked at the front of the stage, David has finally graduated from Fritz to the role of Herr Stahlbaum, and now he is determined to pass on the experience. On stage left, Drosselmeier has reattached the nutcracker head, securing it with his handkerchief while Clara clasps her hands in anticipation.

But really, all eyes are still on me. Herr Stahlbaum turns me around and bends me at the waist. He delivers three hard thwacks, harder than anything he did in rehearsal. It's loud enough for the people in the last row to hear.

"Yay!" screams a little kid, happy that justice has been delivered.

I'm happy too. I can still feel the audience. They are still watching to see what I will do next.

Now that I have the audience's eye, I'm not about to give it up. My job is to annoy Clara. As soon as the music tells me to, I lunge for the nutcracker again.

But this time, Dee Bee grabs the doll from the littlest cousin and smacks me over the head with it. This is not something we rehearsed, and I freeze at her improvisation. Then she reaches over and with one swift tug, unties my perfect silk bow.

Perfect little Clara has retaliated. This is war.

Inspiration ignites through our collective brains like a string of lights on the Christmas tree. All eight cousins get the same idea at the same time.

We have license to misbehave as we have never misbehaved in our lives.

Eight precocious and talented twelve-year-olds who always do their homework and always listen and obey. And right now, we are supposed to be children who are completely out of control.

Two cousins fight over a doll. Sofia grabs a drumstick from her brother and threatens to poke him in the eye. Gone are the straight backs and sucked-in stomachs.

In our normal day-to-day lives, we know exactly where the limits are. We know at what point we will be counted tardy. We know how many problems we need to get right in order to get an A. Being good, being obedient, is like respecting an invisible edge and then getting praise for not going past it.

But here's what Dee Bee already knows: Being onstage is different from being obedient. The edge is so far away, in the distance.

I reach over and grab one of Clara's Nellie Oleson curls as she raises a foot and stomps on my toes.

We are still fighting when the stage parents enter, and now the entire party scene is filled with life. Outraged parents take their children by the ear or the arm. They wag fingers and shake heads.

Mr. Chavez waves his baton and leads the strings through three escalating waves as the timpani drums ripple a warning. It's time to line up for the "Grandfather Dance." Clara is my partner. After all that fighting, it feels too early for a reconciliation. But the music is grand and solemn, telling us that we must be on our best behavior again, even if we don't feel like it. And Ms. Heuser's choreography tells us we must be all the way downstage in front of the other dancers, sharing center.

I pull on the lapels of my jacket and offer Clara my hand. As I do, I think, *I'm sorry. I'm better now. I don't really hate you.*

Dee Bee glows with the same happy look she gives me when she shares her watermelon-flavored Hubba Bubba bubblegum. It's as if she's saying, *I know. Let's dance.*

And then I get it.

This is not about pushing people out of the way. But it's not about being "nice" either. It's about filling the space. Dee Bee fills the space because she is Clara and she is cute and she knows how to act like a little girl on the verge of an adventure on Christmas Eve. My role is different, as is Sofia's, but the challenge to fill the space is the same.

And tonight we filled it. We are dancers.

CLARA GETS A GIFT
AND HER WORLD GROWS

IN A COVETED CORNER SUITE IN THE RESIDENCE DORMS, ONE OF the California girls danced on top of a desk she'd pushed in front of her door. Her earrings were long. Her hair was short, tied up in a black rag, which I recognized as silk. She wore bangles on her arm like Madonna in the "Lucky Star" video and she writhed to Prince, pretending not to notice the rest of us as we dragged our suitcases to our rooms.

The California girls came from places I only knew from television—Malibu, Hollywood, Beverly Hills—and so many beaches: Long Beach, Huntington Beach, Laguna, Newport, Pismo. Their fathers were movie directors or entertainment lawyers. There were two Alisons, three Heathers, and a baker's dozen of Jennifers.

But there was only one Dee Bee. Only one Sofia. Only one Janine. The three of us had scholarships for San Francisco Ballet School's six-week summer intensive, like the generation of Ms. Heuser's dancers before us and the generation before them. We were thirteen years old.

Summer in San Francisco was nothing like the scorching heat in El Paso, where we could actually fry eggs on the hoods of cars. Desert air was dry and empty. There was nothing to hold on to. But here, July was cold. The fog was salty. The air was so full of mist it was almost as though I could reach out and grab it. If this was what summer could be, then anything was possible in this city.

Back home, there were hints of a coup. The ballet master Ms. Heuser had hired from the Royal Ballet was thick and dashing. His feet were arched, as were his eyebrows. He delivered his insults as if they were punchlines. Everyone was in love with him. All the boys. All the girls. Even Renée. He floated through the halls of UTEP like the combination of the Pied Piper and Mr. Darcy from my stepmom's worn VHS tape of *Pride and Prejudice*. There were whispers that he should be the director of Ballet El Paso, not Ingeborg Heuser. Some dancers talked to the board of directors. Others talked to newspaper reporters. It felt like a chess game.

The 29 Sunset bus coughed and sputtered as it wound its way through Golden Gate Park to San Francisco Ballet's studios on Geary Street. When it hit the hills, I could see the Pacific Ocean in the distance. In San Francisco, the houses were skinny and long. They stood shoulder-to-shoulder like books on a shelf. There were no front lawns, just gray concrete that matched the sky.

Sofia and I sat on hard orange plastic seats and waited to tug on the string that signaled the bus to stop. Overhead signs spelled out rules and offered advice. Don't eat. Don't drink. Don't smoke. Don't worry: you can't get AIDS from a toilet seat.

"Oh my gawd! Gag me with a spoon."

The California girls wore designer labels like GUESS and ESPRIT—which, it turned out, was pronounced "e-SPREE" and not "ESS-prit." They wore Vans, Converse high-tops, and Doc Martens. Good things were "totally tubular." Bad ones were "grody."

But in the ballet studio, which smelled like old damp wood (grody) and new paint (also grody), we were dressed the same in black leotards and pink tights. I could see right away that these other girls didn't know anything. They were teachers' pets from their local studios. They didn't know the difference between competing for attention and vying for approval because they'd never had to fight for either. They didn't know how to catch a teacher's eye from the sidelines or how to dance past their mistakes.

And their manners were terrible.

When the teacher entered the room, they stayed sitting on the floor when they should have stood up. When she demonstrated the combination, they stood still when they should have danced. And when class was over, they left when they should have stayed and thanked her.

Dee Bee and Sofia were in the level above mine, so in my class, I was the only one who stood to greet the teacher at the start, the only one who curtsied to her at the end. For the first time, it didn't matter that I went to the left when Ms. Perry demonstrated to the right, because I was the only one dancing the combinations full out. By the end of the first week, Ms. Perry had taken to addressing me directly when she called out the steps, as if I were the only person in the class. It had never been so easy to be the only one.

The other girls weren't mean. They were just a bit clueless. It wasn't their fault that they didn't know how to use hunger to their advantage. They had never been hungry.

Before our first pointe class, I sat on the floor and taped my toes with masking tape. It was much cheaper than toe tape, especially since Sofia and I shared a roll. I tried not to gawk at the girls who stuffed their shoes with toe pads and lambs' wool and used Band-Aids. Renée didn't allow us to wear lambs' wool, let alone toe pads, and of course, neither did Ms. Heuser. And who could afford to go through so many Band-Aids every day? As a result, our feet were stronger and tougher. Dee Bee and I could even stand on the tips of our toes without any pointe shoes at all. Not for very long, but for a bit.

Heather cast a funny glance at my shoes. They were Capezio Infinitas, which were like the Datsuns of pointe shoes. But that wasn't why she stared at them. She stared because my shoes had funny brown spots on them. Obviously, Heather had never had to cook her pointe shoes in the oven to make them last longer. It was a trick that everyone at Ballet El Paso used. Even Renée. If I poured Future floor wax into the tips of the shoes before cooking (two hundred degrees for twenty minutes or until the smoke alarm went off), they lasted even longer. The problem—other than the occasional rash from contact with the floor wax—was that sometimes cooking the shoes made the ribbons crunchy and hard to tie.

The other problem was that Future floor wax only worked to make the tips of the shoes harder. It didn't do anything to reinforce the shank of the shoes, which was where the support for the arch came from. When the shank broke, the shoes were pretty much useless. But I had a trick for this too. I switched my left and right shoes to keep the sole from breaking in the same place, and I rotated pairs to make them last longer. It worked for the moment, but I wasn't sure how I would make it the full six weeks.

Heather's pointe shoes—like almost everybody else's here—were Freeds of London. Handmade by real cobblers called "makers," Freeds were the shoes the professionals wore. Some dancers even had special orders for their shoes—satin cut to specifications perfectly tailored for their toes by their preferred makers, who stamped their mark into the leather soles of the shoes. Some makers' stamps were letters. Others were symbols. Rabbit's Teeth. Triangle en Pointe. Spade. Bell. Clover. Freeds fit better than other brands. With Freeds, dancers balanced longer. They turned more. Freeds made feet look more arched. They even had their own shade of pink, a peachy color known as "Freed pink." The problem with Freeds was that they cost more than other pointe shoes, and they didn't last as long. There was no way my family could afford Freed pointe shoes.

In the dorms, Dee Bee splattered a standard-issue dorm pillow-case with fabric paint she'd brought from home. As generous with her paints as she was with her bubblegum, she showed Sofia and me how to use the bristles of a toothbrush to create patterns. Then she took a seam ripper and cut holes on three sides. Now it was a shirt. It was cooler than anything from the ESPRIT outlet. Cooler even than anything in *Seventeen* magazine. It looked like fashion that hadn't been invented yet.

The other girls swarmed around her, and within twenty minutes, everyone on our floor had painted their pillowcases to look like ours. But they cut their armholes too low or too big. When they put on their shirts, they did not look cooler than *Seventeen* magazine. They looked as if they were wearing bags with drips of junky paint.

They wore them anyway.

In ballet history, we learned that San Francisco Ballet was founded in 1933 by the Christensen brothers Harold, Willam, and Lew. It was the oldest ballet company in the United States, older than American Ballet Theatre by six years and older than New York City Ballet by fifteen—news that made us cheer. SFB was also the first US ballet company to stage a full-length production of *The Nutcracker*. Lew Christensen's wife, Gisella, had been the first Sugar Plum Fairy, and Jocelyn Vollmar, who taught Sofia and Dee Bee in Level 5, had been the first Snow Queen.

But other than that, ballet history was full of archaic minutiae, such as who did what and who taught whom. In a game of call and response, we recited back to the teacher the name of the ballerina who first danced in pointe shoes (Marie Taglioni); the name of the Danish choreographer, as there was only one (August Bournonville); and the contributions of Marius Petipa (choreographer of *Swan Lake* and *Sleeping Beauty*). It was boring to the max.

It feels important to mention what was omitted from our ballet history classes: the three Christensen brothers got their start in vaudeville, and Harold had opened a ballet school in Portland, Oregon, before making his way to San Francisco.

Ballet history would have been more interesting if we had been told juicy stories. For example, for the first *Nutcracker*, Gisella and Jocelyn had to make their own costumes and their own tights, sewing pennies into the waistband because elastic was hard to come by. They had to stand in line for fabric rations limited to ten yards apiece and tore up old theater curtains to repurpose the red velvet. Pointe shoes, made from rubber and leather—both rationed materials—could only be purchased through "shoe stamps." Because Americans were limited to three pairs of shoes a year, dancers supplemented their supply with coupons scraped together from housebound seniors who didn't suffer from footwear scarcity. And because Lew Christensen and the other male ballet dancers had been shipped off to Europe to fight in World War II, his brother Willam recruited football players from local high schools, promising proximity to women to lure them onto the stage.

Perhaps we weren't told these stories because it was the wrong kind of hard work. And maybe I would have been disappointed to hear that San Francisco Ballet, like Ms. Heuser's Ballet El Paso, also had humble beginnings.

For homework, we had to trace our roots back to the very first patron of ballet, King Louis XIV, who loved to dance so much he formed the Paris Opera Ballet in 1669. Most of the girls in my class took the easy route through Lew Christensen and our San Francisco Ballet teachers (although not by way of vaudeville), but Sofia, Dee Bee, and I were linked directly to Moscow and Paris through Ms. Heuser's mentor, Tatjana Gsovsky. If ballet were an inclusive club to which admittance was granted through the legacy of mentor to protégée, we were already members.

One Saturday afternoon, Sofia ran a hand through her long hair and sighed. "I wish I had a bob. But I want it short on one side and long on the other."

"I can do that," I said.

I had never cut hair before. But how hard could it be?

We set up in the hall bathroom. The entire floor gathered to watch us, jostling in the doorway for the best view. I wrapped a towel around Sofia's neck the way my mother did when she trimmed my hair in the kitchen.

With a wet comb, I divided her hair into sections, running

each segment between two fingers as if I were smoothing a pointe-shoe ribbon.

At home, my mother trimmed my hair with long, skinny silver shears like the ones at Supercuts, and the process took less than fifteen minutes. But my scissors were made for cutting ribbons and thread, and Sofia's hair was thick and slippery. Even when I lined up the blade evenly, the hair cut in a jagged line. Locks fell to the ground in clumps.

"How do you know what to do?" asked one of the Jennifers.

"What if you mess up? Aren't you totally freaking out?" asked a different Jennifer.

I shrugged with the confidence I had learned to fake from years of dancing for Ms. Heuser—in spite of her, not because of her.

"It's just hair," I replied.

Forty-five minutes later I was still cutting. It was a good thing Sofia wanted it uneven.

When I finished, her hair barely covered her right earlobe, swooping across the nape of her neck to brush the top of her left shoulder.

Sofia shook her head like a wet dog drying off and looked in the mirror. She looked sleek, like Zola, the only teacher at San Francisco Ballet School we were allowed to address by first name.

She looked every bit like the kind of dancer who would get invited to stay for the year.

"It's perfect," she said.

Meanwhile in El Paso, just when it looked as if Ms. Heuser was cornered, she upended the game board and fired all the dancers in her company. She talked to the newspapers too. She was grief-stricken, she said. She had no choice. It was time for her dancers to leave the nest.

Renée eloped with her Prince Charming. In her letters, she told me that maybe they would go back to London. Or maybe they would be the new directors in Arkansas. The only thing for certain was that she was gone.

"You can't keep wearing those shoes." Ms. Perry looked at the crispy brown ribbons of my Capezio Infinitas, which were the perfect shade for a roasted turkey. "Don't you have any Freeds?"

I shook my head. Ms. Perry sighed, almost exasperated. For a moment, I was afraid she was going to yell at me.

"You look like a four. Wait here."

Instead of her usual brisk walk, she slithered out of the studio and down the hall as if she were planning a sneak attack. She whispered to one of the company dancers. The dancer nodded, disappeared. When she returned, the handoff was smooth, like a drug deal.

Ms. Perry crept back into the studio. She looked both ways, just like when Princess Leia armed R2-D2 with the Death Star defense plans. I almost expected her to say that I was her only hope.

Instead she said, "Don't tell anybody," as she handed me a narrow plastic bag with a red drawstring.

I could see the telltale peachy pink before I felt the weight of the shoes in my hands. The satin was so shiny it was practically singing.

For a second, my heart resisted. I was the underdog. The one with the burnt pointe shoes who always danced backward. I wasn't the kind of dancer who got lucky breaks. But now, with my own pair of Freed pointe shoes, maybe I was.

I knew anything was possible in this place.

BATTLE

OVER A HUNDRED YOUNG DANCERS SAT ON THE FLOOR OF THE Lew Christensen studios on the fourth story of San Francisco Ballet's new building across the street from the War Memorial Opera House. Every student from Level 3 through Level 6 waited to be cast as infantry, cavalry, or battle mice, with three casts of each battalion. It was the longest and most tedious of battle scene rehearsals.

Mr. Gladstein, the tall, thin ballet master, stood at the front of the studio in a white polo shirt and spotless white pants—the kind they call "trousers"—hissing rules through white-fanged teeth.

"If you talk in my rehearsal, you will be asked to leave. If you chew gum in my rehearsal, you will be asked to leave. Illness is the only acceptable reason to miss rehearsal. Exceptions for illness are rarely given. If you need to be sick for any reason—don't."

Robert Gladstein's reputation was legendary. Unlike Ms. Heuser, whose insults were intended to motivate, his were aimed to humiliate, and it gave him pleasure to do so. Dancers hated him with the white-hot intensity of a thousand suns. There is only one person I knew who adored him—perhaps because she danced lead roles in many of the fifty pieces he choreographed for the ballet and opera. She insisted that when Robert Gladstein liked a dancer, he was the truest of allies, fighting to give them the roles they deserved. But today it only looked like he was fighting the urge to smile as he told us all the ways he could ask us to leave rehearsal.

Mr. Gladstein's rehearsal assistant paced back and forth with a clipboard. I didn't know what notes she could be writing. These rules were nothing new. It had never been acceptable to talk, chew gum, or be sick. Just like we were not allowed to have short hair—not even bangs—or wear earrings longer than a half an inch.

"I hope we get paid for this," Rachel murmured. "In our rehearsal for 'Waltz of the Flowers,' they said we'd get, like, ten bucks a show."

"Everybody gets paid," whispered Lisa. "Last year when I was Clara—"

Mr. Gladstein whirled around and pointed to the sea of black leotards. "You think the rules don't apply to you?" He pointed to the girl sandwiched between Rachel and Lisa.

The girl turned bright red and pointed to herself.

"Yes, you. I said no talking. Take your things and go."

There was no use in proclaiming her innocence. Mr. Gladstein was not the sort of person to admit he'd made a mistake, and both this year's Flower and last year's Clara knew better than to confess. The girl swallowed hard and looked down at the floor. She picked up her dance bag and left the studio.

Mr. Gladstein turned to the rest of us. "Any other chatter-boxes here today?"

Silence.

The only other confrontation during the rest of the three-hour rehearsal was the staged skirmish between mice and soldiers.

Because I was short, I was cast as an infantry soldier. If I were back in El Paso, I'd be a waltz flower again, a snowflake, and maybe even Fritz for the fourth year in a row. I'd have grease paint on my face and calamine lotion on my shoes, both of which I now knew were antiquated theater affectations. And each rehearsal in El Paso would have been a battle, a fight for approval. If Ms. Heuser did praise me, it would only be so that she could put down someone else. The comments meant for me would be insults. ("You have to go all the way to San Francisco to have someone tell you to pull in your stomach?") After three years in the summer program here at San Francisco Ballet School, I had made the leap to be a year-round student. I didn't care that I was one of the oldest dancers in Level 5. I was at San Franfuckingcisco Ballet. On scholarship. I was never going back to El Paso. I was done fighting that duel.

Weak afternoon light spilled into the ballet studio through floor-to-ceiling windows while floor-to-ceiling mirrors reflected our imperfections back to us. We stood at the barre in fifth position, heels contorted forward, knees to the side. No nail polish. No dangling earrings. No stray hairs. Twenty students in identical black leotards and the same brand of pink tights trying to do the same steps at the same time in the same way and still stand out. I couldn't hope to be the best ballet dancer at San Francisco Ballet School, but I had the next best thing: a perfect leotard for pas de deux.

A good pas de deux leotard needed to have sleeves. (You didn't want your partner looking at your armpit stubble.) It had to have the proper décolletage (which varied depending on the partner), and it couldn't ride up your butt during repeated lifts and jumps.

Every Friday afternoon we lined up by height—girls on one side, boys on the other. If I edged toward the taller end of the short girls, I knew I'd get paired with Joe, the second-cutest straight guy in the school.

On Mr. Berg's signal, the pianist launched into a series of bored arpeggios, and class began. The girls stood en pointe in fifth position, our body weight resting on two square inches of floor while the boys planted their hands on our waists. They shifted us forward and back, left to right, trying to find the point of perfect balance.

With some partners—the ones who were too young, the ones who were already getting laid, or the ones who didn't fancy girls to begin with—the air was empty. Our bodies were slick with sweat, but there was no heat. Between combinations, the boys would withdraw their hands, and I'd turn my back. But when I danced with Joe, the air was thickly charged with the thrill of physical intimacy. We didn't talk; we barely even made eye contact. But on Fridays, our bodies danced around each other, literally and figuratively.

Joe placed the tips of his fingers on my floating ribs, a few inches from my bra line. He gently pushed me off my balance and then back to fifth position. I could feel my center of gravity connect with the warmth of his palms as we worked together to find equilibrium in incremental movements.

He sneaked a peek down the front of my leotard when I leaned into arabesque. Later, I felt his breath on my neck before our shoulder sit, and it made me tingle. After the music stopped, his hands lingered just a bit longer than necessary.

At the end of class, we murmured our thanks and went our separate ways.

✳

No one else knew that over the summer there had been a party, and afterward, I'd spent the night in Joe's dorm room.

In a Victorian flat in the hills overlooking the Castro, Sofia had thrown herself a goodbye party. It was a garden-variety party by the standards of sixteen-year-old ballet dancers. Bartles & Jaymes. Bacardi and New Coke. Clove cigarettes and Twizzlers to a soundtrack of Simple Minds and the Police. We played the usual drinking games: pirouette competitions and balancing contests, our judgment impaired and confidence bolstered by shots of Smirnoff.

Someone opened a window, and it seemed like a good idea to climb onto the neighbor's roof. Joe, who'd just arrived that morning from the School of American Ballet, crawled out of the kitchen behind me. Summer programs didn't usually let dancers drop into the middle of a session, but San Francisco Ballet had made an exception for him.

I steadied myself on the apex, and Joe sat next to me. I couldn't look at him without blushing. It made my chest freeze.

I couldn't tell if I felt fuzzy from the Bacardi or if I felt brave because I was sitting on the roof—I'd always been good with heights.

In my most confident and matter-of-fact voice, I said, "I know all about you. You're an Aries from Southern California and you just got back from New York."

Joe did not look surprised. Maybe he was also good with heights.

"I know about you too," he said. "You were in Level 5 last summer."

"You never talked to me."

"But I still knew who you were," he answered, tracing the back of my hand with his fingertips.

"Oh," I said, so softly it sounded like a gasp. My chest wasn't frozen anymore. It was quivering.

Joe slipped his arm around my waist, and I turned to face him, the same way I might let a partner guide me through an arabesque promenade. We leaned toward each other until we touched foreheads, like a reverse game of chicken. The tension of his breath on my lips was deafening. Through jumbled senses, I heard electric sparks and saw heat rising off our bodies, even though my eyes were closed. Somewhere in the middle of the throbbing, we kissed—slowly, like a question.

It wasn't my first French kiss. But neither one of those other kisses felt anything like this. Those had been grabby and frenetic. This kiss was supple and pliant, the way we were supposed to move our bodies in Zola's adagio combinations.

And it was a long kiss.

We kissed on the roof, in the hallway, on the sidewalk outside the party, and against a grimy wall in the MUNI station waiting for the M to take us back to the dorms.

We stopped kissing long enough to realize we'd missed curfew, but I knew which stairways were left unlocked. I also knew Joe was the only person that summer who didn't have a roommate. We parted ways in the hall, but after a minute, I tiptoed back to the room I knew was his and knocked on the door.

Joe had already seen me laid bare in my leotard and tights, just as I'd seen him in his skintight white T-shirt and black tights over a dance belt. It seemed there'd be little left to imagine.

I led him over to the narrow dormitory daybed and lay down as if I knew what to do next, and he lay down next to me. I still couldn't believe I was making out with the second-cutest straight guy at San Francisco Ballet School. Not Rachel, who could lift her leg to her ear, or Shiloh, who did triple pirouettes en pointe. Me. Janine from Level 5.

"You knew me?" I asked again.

Joe looked confused for a moment, then whispered, "Of course."

Blue light leaked in through curtainless windows, and I pretended it was moonlight instead of a streetlamp. It cast shadows on Joe's face. His smile was a little lopsided as he worked his way from my chin to my belly, each kiss like a button. A countdown of tiny, exploding supernovas.

At the waistline of my shorts, he hesitated.

"I've never . . . ," I began, which Joe took as a signal to stop. I saw relief on his face, and I knew I'd said the right thing.

Just before dawn, I crept back to my own room.

I avoided Joe for the rest of the summer, terrified of what would happen next. Besides, I was still committing that night to memory—recording our moves the way I'd mentally rehearse a new ballet. I replayed the line of kisses down my neck, the angle of our bodies, the tremors that he had coaxed to the surface with each caress. I wasn't ready for new choreography yet.

Pas de deux was my chance to be near him. In a safe, scripted kind of chemistry, I would feel his hands along my back for a press lift. They circled my waist in a partnered pirouette and cradled the inside of my thigh for an arabesque presságe. As we danced, I could feel his gaze tracing the seams on the back of my leotard. It was almost as exciting as making out.

He wasn't just tracking my every movement because it was

his job. On the outside, I expanded through my fingers and toes, but on the inside, I played with the magnetic space between our limbs. I was both the sun that extends its rays and the flame that calls the moth. I didn't know exactly what I was doing. But I knew I was doing it on purpose.

Summers at San Francisco Ballet School were fun. Students descended on the Franklin Street studios, making it feel more like a beach overrun with tourists than an elite ballet school.

The year-round program was different. Unspoken lists of expectations hung in the air. Every day we were measured against our future selves, which meant that every day we fell short. Our teachers didn't have to tell us we weren't good enough. We knew it already.

Everybody was terrible at something. Jennifer was tall and graceful, but she didn't have a killer instinct. She never pushed to prove herself to the teachers, which worked against her. Maureen was thin, but months of laxatives had made her so weak she could barely lift her leg. Lisa's torso was too long. Patrick was stiff. In the upper levels, the standards were even higher, the margin for error even less. There, it was a different Jennifer who didn't have a killer instinct. It was Siobhan who was too weak from laxatives, Heather who didn't have the right proportions.

There were so many ways to be a failure.

As for me, my neck was short. My ribs were wide. I was browner than everybody else. I was also the only one in my class who had to wear a bra for support, and I spent much of that year pretending I wasn't humiliated by this.

At my high school in El Paso, I had been known as "The

Dancer. The one who went to San Francisco." When I was onstage back home, a light from my heart shone through my bones like sunbeams. I could feel it. But here I was just like everybody else— another teenager who'd moved away from home to pursue dreams of dancing. My shine didn't matter, not unless I was the most flexible or the best jumper or the dancer with the most pirouettes. And I was not.

To ensure we had time to concentrate on our ballet classes, San Francisco Ballet created an academic program. We never even had to leave the building. Our English teacher—double cast as the school registrar—thought it would be a fun assignment for the students to write about a *Nutcracker* experience we'd had. The best three essays from each grade were printed in the program. No one could pick me out of Clara's army, but they would see my byline and read about the time a small Texas ballet company went on tour, and how, when the bus was sidelined with a flat tire, the director discovered she had left behind *The Nutcracker* tapes on the passenger seat of her car.

I knew how the story read to a sophisticated San Francisco audience: a scrappy ballet troupe from a Podunk town tries to put a *Nutcracker* together. And I refused to feel guilty about poking fun at my hometown. It was a good story. That was my killer instinct. I saw my chance to stand out, and I took it.

Only students who danced in the performance could pass the threshold at the artists' entrance at the back of the War Memorial Opera House. After we greeted the guard and signed in, we trudged to the dressing room we shared with Level 4. In El Paso, we would have roamed the halls or watched from the wings. But in San Francisco, we were only allowed to leave to go to the makeup room to get soldier's cheeks painted on our faces, and to the stage when it was time to dance. To ensure our internment, the entrance was guarded by two unpleasant mole women who seemed to have nothing better to do than to glare and fasten costumes.

We still found excuses to leave. My roommate discovered early in the run of thirty-three performances that needing to go to the dressing rooms of the upper levels under the guise of procuring a tampon was particularly effective. She had an unusually long cycle that winter.

But mostly we behaved. We applied our foundation (Max Factor Pan Stik, not Ms. Heuser's grease paint). We waited in line for the makeup artists to apply the finishing touches. Company dancers got to skip the line: the ballerina doll, the candy cane from the Russian variation, the Arabian princess.

Being onstage at the War Memorial Opera House felt as though there were a black hole between the performers and the audience. In El Paso, I felt tethered to the crowd. I soaked in their attention the way a sunbather basks in the sun. When I broke the nutcracker as Fritz, I knew the audience was watching me. When Clara danced, I knew they weren't.

San Francisco Ballet's battle scene was choreographed chaos. Maybe that was why I couldn't feel the audience. But I knew they were out there. I could hear them clap, and when the cavalry galloped onstage, I could hear them laugh. Meanwhile, my fellow infantry troops and I marched, kneeled, and took theatric aim. Those of us who were not mortally stage-wounded by mice either marched offstage or dragged our fallen soldiers to the wings.

After each performance, I took off my makeup with Pond's cold cream and washed my face with apricot scrub. I doused a few cotton balls with Sea Breeze and swiped them across my cheeks. Jennifer had discovered she could take makeup off with diaper wipes, and this was a revelation in our dressing room. If this were El Paso, I'd be able to leave my towel and makeup tackle box until tomorrow's show, but here we were like campers clearing out of a campsite. Everything had to be packed out.

In the last week of performances, Mr. Gladstein called my house. Soldier #4 from Cast A had diarrhea, and they needed me to fill in.

I couldn't believe my luck. I'd seen this happen in movies, and now it was happening to me. I got The Call. I was going to save tonight's performance as Soldier #4. I grabbed my dance bag and rushed to the opera house.

But when I signed in at the artists' entrance, no one said, "Thank God, you're here!" In fact, nobody said anything at all.

In my dressing room, no one seemed to notice that Soldier #4 from Cast A had been replaced by a soldier from Cast C. They didn't even seem to notice I was a head taller and at least five years older than everyone else. Maybe it was because this was a Level 3 infantry and they didn't keep tabs on each other the same way we did in the upper division. I didn't recognize a single dancer.

When it was time to make our way to the wings, I hung back so I could follow the other battle troops. I'd never gone to the stage by myself, and frankly, I didn't think I could make it to the battlefield without getting lost in the bowels of the opera house.

Onstage, I towered over the rest of my platoon.

They were a mess. Every step was a beat early, and no one stayed in line. I tried to anticipate their timing—that's the job in a corps de ballet. But I was literally marching to a different drummer. Not that it made much of a difference. Quite honestly, if they'd only marched out with seven soldiers instead of eight, the audience wouldn't have noticed.

Otherwise, it was like every other battle. We aimed and fired. The audience laughed at the cavalry. Clara removed her shoe and clocked the Mouse King. The nutcracker came to life as mice and soldiers limped offstage.

In El Paso, the gap would have been noticeable. The dancer who filled in would have been a hero. But not here. In the dressing room, I removed my makeup with a baby wipe and packed out my stuff.

After thirty-two Fridays, Joe asked me out on a date.

We met up at a movie theater near the ballet studio. I wore my favorite outfit: a baggy button-down shirt with big orange roses on it, black leggings, and my Converse high-tops. The canvas dug into my Achilles tendons, and the flat soles made my shins hurt, but I liked the way I looked. It was like something Bananarama would have worn.

Joe and I stood facing each other like amateur actors who'd forgotten their lines, deer caught in each other's headlights. I waited to follow him to our seats, and he waited for me to lead us.

"It's a David Bowie movie," he finally said.

Four seconds passed.

"I like David Bowie," I said.

When it came to words, being awkward came naturally to us.

He paused at the concessions counter, scanning the flat boxes of overpriced candy. It was a wall of everything I wasn't supposed to eat. But still . . . how tantalizing! Junior Mints melting in the palms of our hot hands. A box of yellowy popcorn between our laps, and a super-sized Coke with a single straw to share. Buttery lips and salty fingertips to kiss.

But Joe looked worried. He was clearly not indulging in the same fantasy. Maybe he was tallying up the cost of snacks in addition to the tickets he'd already bought. Or maybe he was counting the calories for me, imagining how heavy I'd be in pas de deux class next Friday after a tub of greasy movie popcorn.

Did he know that every week before our health and wellness class I had an appointment with a nutritionist at St. Francis Hospital?

"I don't want anything," I said with a shrug, as if it didn't matter.

My diet had actually worsened since I started seeing the weight counselor. I hadn't eaten a vegetable in months, unless fried zucchini sticks counted . . .

Smothered in ranch dressing . . .

Washed down with a root beer float in a back booth at Zim's . . .

Several times a week.

And I did count them . . . as "steamed vegetables and a Diet Coke."

Like a kid from juvie who tells her probation officer what he wants to hear, my meal reports were complete fabrications. Under "Breakfast," I'd write "bran muffin," when really I'd eaten two servings of coffee cake. Fettuccine Alfredo was recorded as "plain noodles." The nightly bowls of mint chocolate chip ice cream? Those went unmentioned.

But I never lied about the exercise. Most days I walked to the ballet studio from the flat where I stayed with my host family—a six-mile round trip. And every day after my ballet classes were over, I dutifully rode on the stationary bike in the ballet studio's exercise room. I was only required to ride for thirty minutes, but I always rode longer with the hope that one of the teachers would poke her head in and see how hard I was working. Sometimes I even took an extra ballet class in the evenings to work on my technique. Alas, the only other person I ever saw (besides my roommate, who had the audacity to eat Snickers bars while she waited for me) was Joanna, a first-year corps de ballet member.

I knew it was Weigh-in Day when I got to the dressing room and saw the bulky hospital-grade scale that had been brought down from the company lounge on the third floor to the student dressing rooms. It sat between the lockers like an unwelcome intruder. Weigh-ins at St. Francis took place every Wednesday, but weighins at San Francisco Ballet burst into the schedule like pop quizzes.

After scrambling to pee, my classmates and I removed everything that might lighten the load—bobby pins, earrings, even tampons. I took off my bra and changed into a camisole leotard. Surely it weighed less than my long-sleeved one.

I wasn't stupid. I knew that a bra, four bobby pins, and a pair of gold studs didn't weigh the seven pounds I needed to lose between now and when I stepped on the scale. But that wasn't the point. The point was to show how far I'd go to make my goal—and to be seen doing it. If I couldn't step on the scale with confidence, at least I could hold up my chin knowing I'd done everything in my power that day to weigh as little as possible. Not counting the Burger King french fries I'd wolfed down before class.

We lined up in alphabetical order. Zola calculated our weight while another teacher recorded it on the school roster. The numbers were supposed to be confidential, but everyone knew who passed into the triple digits because the clang of the counterweight echoed through the dressing room like the town crier. When it was my turn, I sucked in my stomach and exhaled all the air from my lungs. Zola adjusted the big counterweight to "100" and nudged the small one past five pounds, then past six. One hundred and seven pounds.

Tap.

One hundred and eight.

Tap.

I should have worn my other tights—the ones with the feet cut out. I should have skipped breakfast this morning. I shouldn't have quenched my thirst after class. Everyone knew that water weight was heavier than regular weight. And, yeah. I probably shouldn't have had those french fries.

Tap.

At a hundred and ten pounds, the counterweight sat suspended in perfect balance. Neither teacher said a word, but I saw one of them mark an "X" next to my name after my weight was recorded. When Lisa took her turn after me, the scales slammed in the opposite direction. Zola quickly tapped the counterweights to a balance, as if she could tell just by glancing that Lisa weighed ninety-two pounds.

"This is not a good trend, Janine," Zola said at the next weigh-in. She jotted down my weight in my chart and clicked her teeth. I'd topped the scales at a hundred and eleven pounds and a half.

I clenched my jaw and stepped off the scale, determined to hide my shame, but I knew. My dance career was over before it had even gotten started.

The weight counselor was sure it would help to talk about my problems, but to do that I might have to confess that the nonfat plain yogurt on my meal chart that I'd claimed to have eaten for breakfast was actually more mint chocolate chip ice cream. If she told the school I'd been cheating on my diet, I might lose my scholarship. My parents would make me come home to El Paso. I wouldn't be the Dancer Who Went to San Francisco. I'd be the One Who Failed.

I didn't want to talk. I just wanted to feel better about my body. I wanted to feel like the light that expressed itself through my muscles and made beauty out of movement was a tangible thing that could be seen and admired. When friends from home asked how things were going, I lied. When Joe called on the phone, I asked my host mother to tell him I wasn't home. On Fridays, I avoided the tall end of the short-girl line to make sure we weren't paired up together.

It wouldn't have helped to know that within a year's time, I'd be onstage at the Kennedy Center. I'd be in another city, enrolled in the school of a different ballet company. On full scholarship, I'd perform with a company grooming me for a professional career. I'd lose all the extra weight too. Maybe it was because I replaced mint chocolate chip with Marlboro Lights, or maybe it was because I finally started eating steamed vegetables and bran muffins.

But I wanted to succeed in San Francisco, not someplace else.

While I was flailing, everyone else's star seemed to be rising. Over the weekend, acceptances for the School of American Ballet had gone out in the mail. Both Jennifers got in. Maureen was accepted for the third summer in a row, and Rachel had been awarded the Capezio scholarship. I hadn't even bothered to audition.

I had worked so hard to be seen, and now all I wanted to do was disappear. I didn't want to go to class, but I would have felt worse hiding in the closet eating more ice cream.

The dancer who stood in front of me at the barre wore cable-knit shorts over black tights and a red-plaid flannel shirt, fashion clearly outside the school uniform. She wore pointe shoes at the barre—something I'd never seen a dancer do. Within a few years, Joanna Berman would become one of San Francisco Ballet's adored prima ballerinas. But on that day, she was just a first-year corps member taking an extra ballet class to work on her technique. If she recognized me from the exercise room, she didn't show it.

She had an electric intensity, as if she were putting energy into the studio and drinking it back as fuel. It wasn't just the position of the feet and knees and index finger. When she came down off pointe, she grew taller in her shoes before she descended. Her fondu didn't just melt; it stretched in five opposite directions. One leg was a foundation while the other one reached and reached before curling back like an octopus tentacle. Her come-hither summons beckoned with legs instead of hands.

When she stood still, it looked as if all the atoms around her were aroused, teasing the space. It wasn't that different from the charged tension between Joe's fingertips and my lips. Or his breath and the nape of my neck. The only difference? There was no partner to play to.

I looked around the studio, expecting to see a roomful of students gawking at the shining diamond who'd come to our class. No one else seemed to notice. Not even Zola. Even more astonishing—it looked as if this first-year corps de ballet dancer didn't care. Other dancers I'd admired were like searchlights in the darkness, reaching out to the audience. This was something different. This dancer was letting her shine out, as if she were the center of her own universe and didn't care what other centers existed. She fed herself through her own grace. She wasn't waiting for anyone's approval.

Watching her, I think, *I can do that. I have a beam of light inside me too. It hides behind my breast, afraid that if I open the aperture of my spotlight, everyone will see me and maybe they'll remember I don't belong. But if I stay closed, I will shrivel and wither. I already know—no one is going to pull me onstage and make me a star, like in the Bruce Springsteen video. And if I count up pounds, pirouettes, and degrees of turnout, I will not succeed there either.*

Perfection wasn't attainable. But this—reaching out, drinking it back like an elixir, becoming my own renewable energy source —this I could do. For the rest of the class—in fondu, développé, tombé pas de bourrée—my center of gravity plugged into a place that was both a force of resistance and a power source, intuition that lived in my body as knowledge.

It was as if my legs were meant to move this way—sensual but strong. I was an electrical force greater than the gravitational force. I was charged protons expanding in opposite directions. Rachel might still have a higher arabesque, but who could say? I was a moving illusion, like the light trails left behind by fireworks on the Fourth of July.

If Zola noticed, she paid me no more attention than she paid to San Francisco Ballet's next rising star.

It didn't matter. Dancing like this couldn't be measured, and this glow was all mine.

THE TRANSFORMATION
OF THE PRINCE

MEANWHILE, IN NEW JERSEY, A COLLEGE SOPHOMORE NAMED Matt stands on a ladder onstage. He takes a crescent wrench from his tool belt and rotates one of a dozen lights into its place on the third electric. The director assesses him from the apron of the stage—two arms, two legs; limber enough to climb a ladder; balanced enough to stay there. This kid will do nicely.

"Hey, we need some extra guys for the kick line," the director says. "Can you help us out?"

It is the ninety-eighth anniversary of the Princeton Triangle Club. Twelve Ivy League undergrads will sing, "I'm Baaaaaad," as a parody to Michael Jackson's hit song as they kick ball change in sheep's clothing. The show is short a couple of tap-dancing sheep for the final number. Ever the team player, Matt agrees.

Discovery #1: Kick ball change is surprisingly difficult for the other eleven sheep in the flock. When the choreographer demonstrates a step to the right, Matt follows. Two sheep bump into him, having gone to the left instead. When they rehearse the next day, the other actors—theater majors who have performed in plays since they were in grade school, who auditioned for these roles and have been rehearsing this number for three weeks—have forgotten their kick ball change, shuffle, turn, step.

But not Matt. He is a tap-dancing savant. The best ram in his row.

Discovery #2: He likes this dancing thing.

"You should take modern dance," the choreographer tells him.

In modern, Matt learns that he can roll and jump and be athletic in the same way he darts and dashes on the basketball court. Only this is different. There's no game to win. It's just Matt trying to roll and jump better than he did yesterday.

"If you really want to be a good modern dancer," the professor tells him, "you should take some ballet classes."

After graduation, Matt moves to New York and enrolls at the Joffrey School of Ballet, where he takes class alongside other dancers at his level. He is twenty-two years old. They are nine. At night, he works the graveyard shift at a prestigious law firm, redlining legal documents. His colleagues are an Irish poet and a graffiti artist.

On his nights off, he goes to shows and grows opinions. Steven Sondheim, Jerome Robbins, Twyla Tharp: geniuses. Eliot Feld: nice job, Baby John. But this Balanchine guy was a mess. If he is so great, why do his ballerinas look so sad when they dance his choreography?

Matt has opinions in the studio too. For example, a good leap should sound like some effort went into it. And tube socks and sweatpants are so much more comfortable than ballet shoes and black tights.

He auditions for Seattle's Pacific Northwest Ballet School in his signature sweats and his Princeton basketball tank top. When he receives a rejection in the mail, he sends an appeal asking them to reconsider. He works really hard, he writes.

It's an ad in a dance magazine for a summer ballet intensive on the outskirts of San Francisco that beckons to him. Like a 1930s starlet waiting to be discovered by Hollywood producers,

Matt comes to California with a suitcase and a dream. He's going to make it here. But just in case, he'll get a temp job with this software company that's just invented a browser for this thing called the World Wide Web. While his roommates from college make their way through law school and accept internships with the UN, Matt racks up addresses of Bay Area ballet studios. Every one of them has a *Nutcracker*. Guys are always in high demand and short supply, especially the ones willing to work hard.

"If you really want to line up gigs," the pas de deux teacher of a ballet school in San Jose tells him, "you need to learn how to partner."

Matt learns how to tell when a ballerina is about to fall off her balance and, more importantly, how to discreetly adjust her. He learns to judge his partner's stability by peeking at her standing leg and how to time his lifts with the deepest part of her plié. He learns that if she doesn't look good, he doesn't look good. And by the way, nobody is looking at him anyway.

Discovery #3: It's almost as easy as being a tap-dancing sheep. Although no one else would say that.

"We need you to be the Nutcracker Prince," the director tells him. "Rehearsals are on Wednesday nights and Saturday afternoons."

And just like that, Matt is a professional ballet dancer.

A PINE FOREST
IN WINTER

THE CONDUCTOR RAISES HIS BATON AND LOWERS IT. CLARA AND HER prince jeté as the French horns and the harp sweep them offstage. The flutes chirp intermittently like the kind of snowflakes to watch from the couch with a cup of hot chocolate. The lights are low. This is a nighttime snowfall.

I stand as close as possible to the downstage wing—a cartoonish pine tree laden with shaded cartoon snow. If my tutu touches it, the canvas leg will sway and the audience will notice. But if I'm too far from it, the audience will see me waiting. If you can see them, they can see you. I'm one of the first snowflakes to enter, and when it's my turn, I jeté onstage, careful to kneel on my mark.

The violins pluck, gradually signaling heavier snowfall. The music climbs and climbs, optimistic, without ambition. By the time they repeat the flute's melody, the storm has begun.

After the steps are memorized, the music takes over. But unlike being in the orchestra, where a musician can play only one instrument at a time, our muscles are bouncing from one melody to the next. For this measure, our pitter-patter is the twinkling of a flute, and in the next moment, our limbs are violins. In this way we are carried by Tchaikovsky.

Our groups of four break into couples of two that join with other couples, like cell division gone wrong. Sometimes we dance the same steps in unison or as mirror images. Sometimes we dance in a canon, like a pitter-patter dancing down a spiral staircase. Like a cloud. A snowstorm.

Our costumes are identical. Our hairpieces, light blue wreaths that circle our buns, are identical. We all have shiny pointe shoes and shiny ribbons. Dancing in the corps de ballet is not like being one of the crowd; it is becoming the crowd.

We dance faster and faster. Bourrées, sautés, piques. The harp. The crash. A lone snowflake signals the final barrage of the storm with her solo of jeté manèges.

Dancing in my blue tutu and soft pointe shoes feels as if I'm inside a fairy tale. I am the best kind of invisible. I want to stay here forever.

White confetti flutters down from the rafters, perfect circles, as if a divine hole-punch is responsible for this blizzard. We bourrée into the final formation officially known as "the mushel." The choir's echoes drift higher and higher as the curtain lowers.

SNOWFLAKES

PACIFIC NORTHWEST BALLET'S WINTER TOUR INCLUDED MINNE-apolis, Seattle, and Vancouver, Canada. On days in which I did not dance in the second act, I had plenty of time to go back to the hotel to grab a nap or a bite to eat before I returned to the theater in the evening to do it all over again.

Sometimes I danced as Snowflake #2, and other times I was #4 or #5. Finally, my tic of dancing to the left when everyone else went to the right had paid off. Years of reversing directions made me a quick study when it came to learning different spots in the corps de ballet, an admirable trait for a *Nutcracker* run of fifty performances sandwiched between Thanksgiving and New Year's. But it didn't mean I'd be offered an apprentice contract, which was all that mattered.

The cast list—a massive grid of lined shelf paper larger than a beach towel—was tacked up next to the sign-in sheet at the artists' entrance. There was a row for each role and a column for every performance. In the intersecting cells, dancers' last names were penciled in director Francia Russell's handwriting, which was as precise as her fifth position and as impeccable as the bun at the nape of her neck.

The cast list wasn't just a record of names and performances.

It was a forecast full of clues. When the corps member who shared the Snow #5 spot with me was selected to dance Clara early in the run last year, it was a vote of confidence. She got promoted to soloist at the end of the season. But when another corps member was asked to learn the coveted Peacock solo and only given one show the entire time we were on tour in Portland, it gave the opposite message. She would leave the company at the end of the year.

Unfortunately, for students like me, the clues weren't so clear. I was nineteen and in my third year in the advanced division of the school at Pacific Northwest Ballet. There were thirty advanced students at PNB. In January, after *Nutcracker* performances were over, we'd get more direct hints about our futures during our annual conferences. Most of us would be told we could stay in the school with the justification that we couldn't advance to the company because we were either too weak or needed to lose five pounds. But the older ones, like me, would be "invited" to audition elsewhere, which was code for rejection. Only one or two students would be given contracts as apprentices.

Seattle had grown on me these last few years. I loved that I got to dance with the company in corps de ballet roles. I would have never had this opportunity in San Francisco. I loved that there were so many *Nutcracker* performances that I'd lose track of what day it was. I loved the sacrifice disguised as glamour. It made me feel like a real dancer.

I could see myself settled here, dancing this *Nutcracker* with its sets by Maurice Sendak, moving up in the ranks from Little Flower to Ballerina Doll. I wanted to be one of the dancers at the center barre in ragged leg warmers and a coffee-stained T-shirt and plastic pants instead of the uniform the students had to wear. I was tired of begging the company girls for their discarded pointe shoes, which my friends and I greedily collected, not as souvenirs but to wear as our own and squeeze out just a few more minutes of pointe work from them. Better yet, I wanted my own special-order Freeds.

But there was the problem of my current boyfriend, a jazz guitarist who thought ballet was the kind of thing one did in the kitchen while washing dishes. It wasn't a real job. Similarly, I thought jazz music was the kind of thing that played in the background while people ate in diners or rode in elevators. It wasn't real music.

In addition to our artistic differences, we were embarrassed of each other. I looked too young to be nineteen, he looked too old to be twenty-seven, and the disapproving stares of strangers mortified him. I was embarrassed because his knees turned inward. And his feet were flat! I would have died if anyone at Pacific Northwest Ballet knew that I was living with a guy with who had flat feet.

My gray-haired, knocked-kneed, flat-footed boyfriend moped more than he yelled, and he yelled way more than he hit—that was a plus. Furthermore, all that yelling meant that I got to yell back, which was new for me. As Sofia would say, we're good with scraps. We're efficient that way.

There was a small voice in my head that tried to remind me this was not the way nice people treated each other. But if I started to listen to that voice, it would never shut up. It would point out that my whole class was injured because the stage was hard and we were young. It would question why even the principal dancer—who had been in Seattle for over ten years and danced all the lead roles—still didn't feel secure in her job. It would whisper it was weird to giggle at the choreographer's crude jokes just to curry favor.

But I hadn't come all this way, all these years, with bleeding feet and strained muscles to give up. Ballet was supposed to be hard, I told the voice. Relationships were supposed to be hard. I took my commitments seriously.

The new year brought the audition season. Photographers needed to be hired for audition shots, but the good ones were expensive, and the cheap ones didn't know how to time the snap of their camera with the apex of a piqué arabesque. Their failure would only be discovered weeks later when the photos had been developed. Résumés needed to be professionally set and sent to the printers on floppy disks. Mine came back with two typos that I corrected with a pencil and my best penmanship.

Everyone knew the best way to get a job was to have an "in." Maybe you danced the director's choreography with another company. Maybe an old roommate was in the corps de ballet and could introduce you to the artistic staff. If so, you skipped the formal audition. You would take class with the company, where the director could size you up alongside his current dancers. But I had a good feeling about this cattle call at Boston Ballet, so I decided to take my chances.

Boston Ballet—where Joe had been dancing for the last two years—was a union company like Seattle. This meant dancers got health insurance for the thirty weeks of the seasonal contracts and unemployment insurance for the rest of the year. It meant they couldn't work ten hours a day or be fired without proper notice. Most of all, it meant they didn't have to buy their own pointe shoes.

Boston looked like a nice town. I wasn't sure how I would weather the winters, but I could call it home. If I got a job there, I'd break up with my boyfriend. Maybe Joe and I would get back together.

At the audition, three hundred dancers smushed into a studio built for fifty. Four ballet mistresses paced the length of the barres writing notes on clipboards. Every few combinations, cuts were announced and dancers left. My legs felt heavy—like slushy January snow that hadn't fully melted. In the center, I went to the right just like everybody else. But I still got cut after the petite allegro. Everyone else was taller, thinner, younger, and still somehow more experienced. Later Joe told me that there were three dancers left at the end of the audition. They talked to one of them. They hired someone else. Someone who had come to class the following week.

"They never take people from those auditions," he said. "They only hold them because the union requires it."

In Washington, DC, which was not union and had a much shorter season than Boston or Seattle, I arranged a private audition in the form of company class. This meant instead of finding out from a friend that they would hire someone else, the director— a dead ringer for Ms. Heuser but with hair dyed black instead of red—told it to my face. There was even a trace of a smirk as she told me she could not hire me.

Portland, Oregon, had two ballet companies. I auditioned for both. One company offered me an apprenticeship that paid $300 a week for a season of twelve weeks. I'd make more money living rent free in my hometown and dancing for Ballet El Paso.

At the other company, I auditioned through company class,

and afterward, the ballet mistress asked me to stay for rehearsal and understudy the corps de ballet roles for *Giselle.* "We might need dancers in the fall. Can you come back tomorrow and talk to the director?"

The next day I arrived at the appointed time and place, only to hear groans and moans from the director's office. Had I been invited to the casting couch only to arrive too late to the party? I entered, clutching my folder of headshots, résumés, and recommendation letters. Inside, the director lay on his back on the floor, knees up, rocking slightly from side to side. His face was beet red, and his moans were loud and guttural.

"He's passing a kidney stone," the ballet mistress said, matter-of-factly, as if this were a normal afternoon activity. I turned to leave.

"It's okay. You can stay. It won't be long. He'll be with you in about ten minutes."

If the director would have preferred a modicum of privacy at this time, he was in too much pain to say so.

The ballet mistress, an admin, and I stood around him in a little semicircle. The admin and ballet mistress were patiently impatient, as if we were waiting for him to finish a phone call rather than pass a pebble-sized renal calculus through his ureter. *I should do something,* I thought. *I should say something. We should call someone. At the very least, we should give this man a moment to himself.* Then again, this could be my one chance for a private interview. I couldn't let this little health issue obstruct my path to becoming a professional dancer. Besides, none of the adults in the room were concerned, so why should I be?

After five minutes of rolling and writhing, the director stood up and walked to his desk, as if we were filming a movie and someone had announced, "Ballet audition, take two. Action!"

His face was pale. Beads of sweat lined his forehead. His nonchalance was noteworthy (and likely a clue as to how he expected his dancers to perform through injuries). He said nothing of kidney stones or pain. He didn't excuse or even acknowledge the time he'd spent on the floor of his office. Instead he looked up at me and down at my résumé. He promised to call if something turned up. Then he sent me home.

There was a rumor that Miami Ballet might be hiring short dancers, but I didn't have the money for the plane ticket. Houston was only hiring soloists.

Finally, a lucky break. News trickled down from last year's crop of ballet students that Fort Worth was looking for dancers. I flew to Texas and stayed with a friend. After a week of classes and rehearsals, the director offered me a job. By the time I arrived back home, a contract had arrived in the mail. But then two days later, the executive director called. They had found someone younger. Could I mail back the contract, unsigned? It was no longer valid.

Meanwhile, in Seattle, I shrank back a little more each day. The voice inside me hissed that I was appreciated for my obedience but not valued. When the cast list was posted for *Swan Lake*, my name wasn't there at all, not even as a third-cast peasant.

My new job came with sick days, vacation days, health insurance, and a free bank account with unlimited ATM withdrawals at all approved locations. I made $6.25 an hour, and all I had to do was answer the phone and help people balance their checking accounts.

I learned things that I imagined normal people already

knew how to do, such as how to tri-fold a letter-sized bank statement so that the customer's address showed through the plastic window of the envelope and how to read microfiche and file it safely after researching. I learned about interest rates and trends, the difference between FDIC and FSLIC insurance, and most importantly, which office supplies could be taken (envelopes, legal pads, Uniball pens) versus which could not (staplers).

At the bank, nobody cared how old I was (except for my boyfriend) or how much I weighed (again, except for my boyfriend).

"I didn't think it would take so long for you to lose those five pounds," he said. It sang like a compliment.

For years I'd stood in front of mirrors, next-to-naked in pink tights and a black leotard, knowing everyone else sized me up too: the thirty dancers in my class, the forty dancers in the company, the director, the school faculty, the costumers, the stagehands, and all three thousand people in the audience, dismissing me as fat or old or weak or not worthy. To have the echo of criticisms reduced to a single voice was a relief.

I still took ballet classes because sitting at a desk all day made me feel like a coiled spring, like a jackrabbit stuck in a box. But now I danced because I wanted to, not for some director's approval. I wore ragged leg warmers and coffee-stained T-shirts. I didn't dance on bloody toes anymore, and my shins never hurt.

I did this for two years.

In the end, it wasn't my boyfriend's weekend tryst with Christine from loan servicing that made me leave, although it did serve as an excellent excuse to smash his favorite plate. It was the voice that pointed out my body hurt again—but only after hours of sitting, never after hours of dancing.

I knew one of Ms. Heuser's old colleagues taught a ballet

workshop in Ghent, Belgium. So as I picked up shards of broken plate, I resolved to open a secret savings account. For the next year, I quietly siphoned off pennies from my paycheck until I had a passport, a plane ticket, and a plan: if I couldn't get a job dancing in the United States, then I would go to Europe. I was ready to do better.

Unfortunately, at my audition in Antwerp, the director had roaming hands. In Dusseldorf, they were on vacation. Essen and Lübeck were only looking for modern dancers, while Bonn had a preference for Russians. However, Hannover needed extra swans in October. Could I come back in the fall?

In Hamburg, my luck began to change. One of the teachers in Ghent thought I would make a good fit for this company, which, with seventy dancers, was larger than San Francisco Ballet or even American Ballet Theater. All over the city, there were posters of the dancers from Hamburg Ballett, even a calendar in the window of a bookstore. Dancers were like rock stars here. When I didn't get lost on the S-Bahn, it felt like a good omen.

For a week, I took class with the company in the morning and with the school in the afternoon. After every class, a teacher would call me over and ask, "Are you here to audition for the company?"

"Good," they'd remark when I answered in the affirmative. "Make sure you come back tomorrow."

The ugly duckling had found her flock.

The official audition lasted five hours in front of a jury of nine faculty members. Three dancers competed for two spots. One of the girls was young, seventeen, maybe. She was willowy and a nondescript sort of blonde. The other dancer looked like me. We both had dark hair and brown skin. I had better technique, but she had more confidence. For class, we danced with the rest of the company but in front of each group, even in front of Gigi Hyatt, the principal dancer whose face graced the sides of newspaper kiosks. Meanwhile, the jurors squinted and scribbled. They nodded or frowned as they whispered to each other.

After class, the company dancers disappeared, and the three of us donned pointe shoes for thirty minutes of pointe work. I was the stronger dancer; I felt it. After a short break, we came back to rehearse with the company, and after that, a private rehearsal where we were shown strange choreography set to strange music. I danced to the left while my doppelgänger danced to the right. She picked up steps faster than I did. I was losing my footing.

In the end, they took the young girl into the school and the other girl into the company. But they still weren't sure about me. Could I stay an extra week?

I could not. I had overstayed my welcome on the couch of friends of friends of friends. I had spent all my cash, including the money earmarked for the Radio Shack credit card that paid for my boyfriend's video game console.

Besides, I was homesick. I thought Germany would have the rolling green hills of Julie Andrews's Austria in the opening credits of *The Sound of Music*, but it was sad and gray, which was really saying something coming from someone who lived in Seattle. And as much as I didn't want to be "that kind of American," after three weeks in Europe, I had to admit that I was. I missed ice cubes in my Coke and English the way I expected it to be spoken. I even missed the texture of the toilet paper at home.

I thought it was a trick of the ear when, walking to my seat in coach, I heard my name called. It came from an old lady in first class who looked surprisingly similar to the only other old German lady I'd ever met. Obviously, I was so homesick for the familiar I'd conjured up a vision of Ms. Heuser on my plane back to the States. I was like the lovesick boyfriend from the rom-coms who sees his beloved ex everywhere.

Except that Ingeborg Heuser was the last person I wanted to see. For starters, I hadn't bathed in three days, and aside from a few Belgian francs and a handful of Deutsche pfennig, I was completely broke. I'd spent the last five hours sitting on the floor of the Frankfurt airport bumming cigarettes off of nice German men and the eight hours before that on the overnight train from Hamburg.

"Janine! What are you doing here?"

I stopped in the aisle, as if I'd been caught.

Of all the airplanes on all the tarmacs in all the world, I had to walk onto this one.

"Go, go. Get settled. Then come back and we can catch up." Ms. Heuser patted the empty seat next to her.

The voice on the plane's intercom—first in English, then in German—asked the passengers for their attention as the flight attendants pantomimed the safety features of the plane that would take us across the ocean to Dallas. This seven-hour flight was supposed to be a sanctuary from my failings, but knowing Ms. Heuser was sitting in the same space clouded everything. I rested my feet on my duffel bag under the seat in front of me and looked out the window.

In the bathroom, I rubbed one hand wipe on my face and used another on my armpits, just the way Rick Steves had recommended for weary travelers short on amenities. I thought about adding makeup but decided against it. I didn't want to look as if I was trying too hard. And besides, between dancing and couch-surfing in the homes of other starving artists, I'd lost over ten pounds. Being skinny would certainly make a bigger difference than a little mascara.

I made my way to first class. Maybe if I timed it right, Ms. Heuser would treat me to lunch.

"What are you doing in Germany?" she asked.

"I came to audition."

"In Germany? *My* Germany?" She looked stunned, which was equally mystifying to me. I'd heard about German companies from her. How did she not think I would follow her advice?

"I auditioned for Neumeier. In Hamburg."

"You didn't! Tell me everything."

"At barre I stood right behind Gigi Hyatt."

Ms. Heuser gasped. "What did she look like?"

I thought for a moment. "Small. Quiet. Like she didn't have anything to prove."

In class, Gigi Hyatt wore mostly pink. She had a quiet kind of grace, like a mist made from cotton candy. And she was nice. I could tell because the other dancers weren't afraid of her.

"What was the studio like?"

In many ways, the building at Hamburg Ballet was like the studios at San Francisco Ballet: the same dotted vinyl panels in the stairwells; the same white bars in the studios; the same grand pianos. But the main studio at Hamburg Ballet was the largest studio I'd ever been in. The walls were exposed brick, and the ceilings looked three stories high. It was part banquet hall and part warehouse. Even the Lew Christensen studios in San Francisco were small compared to this. When the full company took class—nearly seventy dancers—there was enough room for everyone to dance at the same time.

"But I didn't get the job," I said.

"Oh, but you tried! That's the important thing. You took a risk!" she said. "Go, get some rest. When the plane lands, come find me. I called for a wheelchair. You'll push it, and we'll get through customs faster."

The glare from the sun shone through the window and onto her cheek. Past her, I could see the miles of ocean—blue that never stopped. I stood up to leave.

"I'm so proud of you."

I took a moment to grasp this novel concept. I didn't travel to Germany auditioning for ballet companies in order to make her proud of me. I honestly didn't think that was possible. I came because if I was going to take myself seriously and my art seriously, this was the kind of job I wanted.

I now knew it wasn't enough to be good. It wasn't enough to be talented or ambitious. It wasn't enough to have connections. I needed to be brave. And if I couldn't be brave, then I needed to listen to the thing inside me that refused to be silent. I needed to tend to it in the face of doubt or fear or criticism, like stoking a fire. In the dark night of the soul, the thing inside me that refused to be silent was the light.

In E. T. A. Hoffmann's *The Nutcracker and the Mouse King*, there's a side plot that rarely makes it into the ballet versions: The king's astronomer and Drosselmeier, the king's clockmaker, leave the kingdom in search of a magic nut, the Krakatuk, and the hero who can crack it. This is the only way to break Frau Mouserink's spell that has disfigured the princess. If they can't find the nut and the hero, the king will kill them. They search high and low, and finally, after fifteen years, Drosselmeier says, "Screw it. You know, we don't ever have to go back to the king. Let's just go to my cousin's house." Which, as it turns out, is where the Krakatuk and the hero have been the entire time. The astronomer, Drosselmeier, the nephew, and the nut return victorious to transform the princess back into a pretty girl.

It's interesting what Fate hands you when you give up and go home.

But in order to go home to El Paso, I had to tell my boyfriend a few lies. I told him I had given up on ballet. I was just going to El Paso for the weekend. I'd be back before he knew it. I packed my ballet clothes, pointe shoes, and journals. I left my books, photo albums, and video camera. I wasn't sure what he would do if he suspected I would leave him. He wouldn't drive me to the airport—that was for sure.

I didn't expect Ms. Heuser to welcome me, but she did. Perhaps knowing I went to Germany—her Germany—finally made me desirable in her eyes. I danced in "Waltz of the Flowers." In "Spanish Chocolate." In "Chinese Tea." I was even Fritz again. It had been eight years since I had danced in her *Nutcracker,* and little had changed. She still tied my silk tie and saved the best wig for me. ("If it hurts, you know it won't fall off!" she said, still a little too gleefully.)

There was only one dancer for each role—there were not enough of us to have more than one cast. Then again, there were only six performances. My snow costume was blinding white and not subtle blue. The snowflakes in El Paso were tiny chips of Styrofoam that hit the stage with a clatter, as if we were dancing in a hailstorm. The snow didn't fall like confetti the way it did in Seattle.

But many things were exactly the same. The conductor still

raised and lowered his baton. Clara and her prince were still swept offstage by harps and French horns. The flutes chirped. The violins plucked. By the time they repeated the flute's melody, the snowstorm had begun.

Then a postcard arrived in the mail from the teacher in Ghent, now the new ballet master in Iceland. One of their dancers had injured her back, he wrote. *Stay tuned.*

A week later, the phone rang. I almost didn't answer it, afraid it might be my boyfriend, who was now officially my ex-boyfriend.

"Have you been informed about the Icelandic Ballet?" asked a woman with a slight lilt to her English.

Yes, I had. By this postcard of a volcano in the snow.

The woman asked for my passport number and my fax number. Then she hung up.

Twenty minutes later, a fifteen-foot fax rolled into my father's office like a stream of consciousness. The contract from the National Ballet of Iceland had all the standard European terms: thirteen months, including eight weeks of paid vacation in the summer and three weeks' paid vacation in December. Included in the fax was a confirmation number for a one-way plane ticket to Reykjavik and a voucher for three months' rent in a flat downtown. The contract started in the new year after *Nutcracker* performances were over.

Just like that, I was a professional ballet dancer. Who knew it could be so easy.

THE SPACE
BETWEEN ACTS

SEWING KIT CONTENTS:

* 11 needles of varying lengths
* 1 needle threader you have never used
* 16 tiny spools of thread in varying colors
* 1 large spool of red thread
* 1 pair of fold-up scissors that break every time you use them
* 1 seam ripper
* Unwaxed dental floss for darning the tips of Freeds while you watch reruns of *Friends*
* 2 straight razor blades for cutting red cards of pointe-shoe shanks
* Heel of discarded red card, used for measuring
* Tape measure, never used
* 18 elastic drawstrings pulled from old pointe shoes because you never know when you might need skinny elastics

MAKEUP BAG CONTENTS:

* Blue Paper Mate ballpoint pen for fastening hair in French twist
* Hairbands, hairspray, 2 hairnets—1 black with hole too big to be useful, the other white in pristine condition because when would you ever use a white hairnet?
* 1 rock of rosin, swiped from rosin box in Geneva
* 1 pink hand towel, pilfered from hotel room in Salzburg where you expected to stay only one night but had to go back a second night because the consulate needed another day to process your Italian work visa
* 1 Italian aspirin bottle. Contents: 23 bobby pins
* 1 dented Altoids tin. Contents: 4 three-inch German hairpins liberated from your Fritz wig
* 1 shiny Altoids tin. Contents: 9 rhinestone earrings of varying diameters
* 3 validated bus tickets, Verona
* 1 Italian phone card
* Coins: German marks, Italian lire, Belgian francs, American quarters
* 1 box of tampons
* Dark pancake makeup for pointe shoes
* Slightly lighter pancake for face
* 1 pair false eyelashes, the bad ones
* 1 pair false eyelashes, the good ones
* 1 tube of eyelash glue that feels empty but always manages to have just enough glop for one more show
* Gnome from Norwegian pavilion at Epcot Center

* 1 MUNI pass, San Francisco
* 1 cassette tape of *Carmina Burana*
* 1 tube of Superglue for cracked skin
* 1 package corn remover pads

OTHER THEATER ESSENTIALS:

* 1 stack Georgia-Pacific Professional Series 1-Ply C-Fold paper towels, for use in pointe shoes
* 1 box of Band-Aids
* 1 sock with holes in all the right places
* 3 socks with holes in all the wrong places
* Black silk makeup robe with embroidered dragon from Chinatown in Vancouver, Canada
* 1 fold-up hair dryer that always smells like it's short-circuiting
* 1 pair leg warmers knitted from clearance yarn bucket in Graz, Austria, with pointe-shoe elastic drawstrings
* 3 oz. bottle of acrylic cement for emergency pointe-shoe use
* 1 leather cigarette case from Milan with Camel cigarettes from Reno

Twenty pairs of new, special-order Freed pointe shoes, sorted by maker (with a preference for C or M, but G and EE were also acceptable), stood on their tips against the baseboard of my bedroom. Some were already darned with dental floss. Some were already painted to match my skin. All had been treated with acrylic cement to make them last just a bit longer.

The process that brought me back to San Francisco mirrored the one that took me abroad. A ballet master who knew me. A phone call, a contract, a plane ticket.

My apartment sat on the edge of Golden Gate Park. It smelled like old damp wood and new paint. When the 29 Sunset bus sputtered past, my windows shook, but my Freeds stayed suspended in perfect balance.

On a sunny September day in a redwood grove outside Atherton, California, I sat on a white folding chair and waited for the wedding to start. I hadn't been invited, but the bride and I danced together in the same company—Smuin Ballet in San Francisco. It meant we were practically family. If I hadn't just met Amy and her fiancé a week before their nuptials, I was sure I would have had my own invitation. With the same confidence I employed when understudying a leading role for which I had not been cast, I showed up anyway. If Amy was surprised at my boldness, she didn't show it. She simply led me over to the singles table after the vows had been exchanged.

"Janine," she said. "I'd like you to meet someone. This is Matt."

Matt had the quiet confidence of a guy who had a lot of choices. He didn't dress like a dancer. He didn't wear a thrift-store tie or a suit jacket from the costume room. He didn't drink like a dancer either, favoring beer over bourbon. But he talked like a dancer, able to segue any conversation into a self-deprecating anecdote.

"That's like the time I was paid in unitards. I danced the lead in an opera about the solar system. The lyrics were literally 'There are rings around Uranus.'"

We mulled over which indie bands made the best music for a pop ballet and the choreographers who'd comprise our dream repertoire. By the time Amy threw her bouquet, I thought I might have just met the man I was going to marry. That is, if I stayed in San Francisco long enough.

None of my other dancer friends were married. Most dancers I knew changed ballet companies every couple of years. Long-distance relationships were common but rarely lasted. It was too hard for couples to find work together; it was easier to break up. I had left my last boyfriend when I relocated from Italy to dance in San Francisco. Or maybe he'd left me to dance in Scotland. Either way, ballet had been more important than our relationship.

Michael Smuin, who had been the director of San Francisco Ballet when I was a teenager, was the founder of Smuin Ballet. Michael choreographed to the Beatles, Willie Nelson, and Edith Piaf as well as to Bach and Chopin. His ballets were both technically demanding and audience-pleasers. Costumes ranged from tutus to jeans to lingerie.

Smuin Ballet didn't have a *Nutcracker*; instead we danced *The Christmas Ballet*. The first act was costumed in white and choreographed to classical music. The second act was all red and set to popular Christmas songs like Bing Crosby's "White Christmas" and Eartha Kitt's "Santa Baby." There were tap-dancing trees and even an Elvis impersonator.

One of my roles was the Little Surfer Girl in Leon Redbone's

"Christmas Island." My job was to sit on the shoulders of my partner as he stood on a surfboard mounted on a platform.

One day in rehearsal, Michael decided to try something new. What if I stood on my partner's shoulders instead? Could I do that? In ballet companies, if you want to get ahead or just keep your part, the answer is always "yes."

My partner Osmani stripped off his shirt to minimize slippage, and I removed my shoes and rolled up my tights over my calves. Bare skin on bare skin. That seemed safest.

"Try it without the platform," Michael suggested. "Osmani, take her by the waist and lift her onto your shoulders. Now from there take her hands. Can you climb on his shoulders from there?"

I couldn't. Sitting on Osmani's shoulders the way you might play chicken in a swimming pool didn't give me enough leverage to stand.

"Okay, climb up from behind. See if that works."

Osmani crouched down and reached his arms over his head to grab my hands. I tried to climb on his back as if he were a boulder, but it didn't work. I tried again, hoisting one leg up and planting a foot directly on his shoulder, then using the momentum to plant my weight and swing the other leg up. With shaky but strong legs Osmani stood up. I could feel him find his balance, which helped me find my own. I straightened my legs. *This isn't so hard*, I thought.

"That looks great." Michael grinned. "Let's try it on the board."

Osmani climbed onto the surfboard platform and extended a hand. I stood behind him, and we clasped hands.

"Shouldn't someone spot her?" Amy asked.

Michael shook his head. "She's got this," he said with confidence.

I've got this, I repeated to myself. I swung one foot, then the other onto Osmani's shoulders. Beads of perspiration dotted his skin.

Don't look down, I thought, as I did exactly that. I could feel my center of gravity tilt when I did. It made Osmani wobble, which he used to help him wiggle back to a steady stance. His stability became my foundation. Standing tall in my black leotard and tights, I towered over the studio full of dancers, their concentration mirroring mine. I looked straight ahead, pressing down through my feet and pressing my palms into Osmani's. A solid balance feels like a moving current. It's electric.

Osmani bent his elbows as I bent my knees and prepared to dismount. Our hands were sticky.

A dancer should never look at her feet while she is dancing. It breaks the aesthetic line. It also breaks her focus.

The shift of balance was minuscule. A waver. A flicker. Like an absent-minded thought. If I had been able to teeter forward and then back, we might have found our balance again. But when I glanced at my toes sliding off Osmani's chest, now slick with sweat, I had a flash of panic.

My colleagues looked up at me as I started to fall, all of them too far away to help.

My mind flipped through the various possible scenarios. I pictured Osmani twisting on the narrow surface of the platform, contorting to catch me, his back breaking on the edge as we both toppled. I imagined him shifting to keep his balance, but falling on one foot, knee cracking as we both crashed to the floor. I envisioned myself falling forward, puncturing my sternum on the edge of the board. I saw myself falling into his arms, helpless like a fish flopping on the shore, taking him down with me.

As soon as you imagine that you are falling, you fall.

If only I'd had the courage to say, "I'm not sure what I'm

doing." If only I'd been able to find the eye of the storm within my balance. If only we'd had someone spotting us. If only I hadn't imagined falling.

I pushed off Osmani's chest as if it were a diving board, and he thrust my feet forward on a diagonal, propelling me past the edge of the board.

They say I flew.

I soared through the air like an acrobat. I landed on my face in a collapsed push-up. My legs bent back over my head. I never braced for impact.

If there were gasps or shrieks, I didn't hear them.

Someone helped me to my feet. Someone else gave me some water to drink.

"Are you okay?"

"Are you hurt?"

"Do you want to see a doctor?"

"Do you need anything?"

"Do you think you can dance tonight?"

I answered, "Yes," to all the questions.

In the waiting room of the ER, Amy filled out the forms for me. She described the accident: "Fell from a height of twelve feet onto her face."

A nurse checked for broken teeth. A doctor examined me for internal bleeding. The X-ray technician looked for broken bones. Nothing.

"Tell me again how you fell?" The doctor looked at me, puzzled.

After I described the accident, the doctor shook his head. "You could have bitten your tongue or smashed your rib cage." I couldn't tell if he thought it was miraculous or if he thought I was exaggerating. "Yeah, sure. You can dance tonight. Come back if anything changes."

Back at the theater, I was a hero. I'd survived the most stunning of falls and didn't even have a bruise. We changed the lift, of course, but I felt like I was invincible.

ACT II

THE SUGAR PLUM
AND THE CAVALIER

I SAT ACROSS FROM THE DIRECTOR IN A SAN FRANCISCO SUSHI restaurant and accepted the job offer translated to me from Japanese to English. The ballet was *The Nutcracker*. The role was the Sugar Plum Fairy. I hadn't danced the production since I left El Paso.

Airfare to Kyoto and a generous per diem would be provided, but I would have to bring my own partner and my own tutu. I didn't have the tutu, but I did have the guy. We'd never danced together before, but we'd dated for about four months. Or maybe we were still dating, depending on the time charted between phone calls. In that case, we'd been together for a year and a half.

During the day, Matt worked in Silicon Valley as a paralegal for a software company. At night and on weekends, he taught pas de deux class for several ballet studios, often performing in their *Nutcracker*, *Swan Lake*, and spring showcases.

For several months we were inseparable. We went out. We stayed in. We worked favorite movie lines into casual conversation, provoking belly laughs that doubled as an abdominal workout. There was an effortlessness to our time together.

"At this rate, he's going to propose by summer," I said to Sofia.

Then a strange thing happened. A weekend of laughter and intimacy would be followed by a week or two of dead air, like an intermission between acts or the way prima ballerinas rest between performances to prevent injury. Eventually one of us would call. We'd hang out, have fun, and then exit again through separate wings.

The choreography of our relationship was predictable but frustrating. I preferred the endurance test of a marathon of dates, like a *Nutcracker* season of fifty shows crammed between Thanksgiving and New Year's. I was only willing to put in the effort if Matt thought the relationship would last.

I wanted to ask (scream), "What are we doing?"

But I never did. The truth was that at thirty-one, I was transitioning to my next career—whatever that might be. Web programming, perhaps. Or maybe I would finally go to college. I wanted to find out what my life would look like outside of ballet before sharing it with someone else. Besides, after ten years of ballet roommates, I enjoyed the newness of living alone. I couldn't demand a commitment on his part if I wasn't willing to do the same. The gig in Japan was a perfect way to put a few more dates on the books without showing my hand or asking for his.

Between Ballet El Paso, San Francisco Ballet, and Pacific Northwest Ballet, I'd been Fritz, a soldier, a warrior mouse, one of Mother Ginger's buffoons, and a party guest. As a professional, I'd danced as a snowflake shimmering in the lightest possible shade of blue, as a flower waltzing in pastels of layered tulle, and as every flavor of candy in the Land of the Sweets. But I'd never been the Sugar Plum Fairy. I didn't even know the choreography. Matt promised to teach me his favorite version.

He unlocked the doors to the ballet school where he taught pas de deux class on Thursday nights. As we warmed up on opposite sides of the studio, I imagined our upcoming trip. Me, falling asleep on his shoulder as we shared headphones on the plane. Perhaps there'd be a bowl of fruit on the table of the apartment where we'd stay. Maybe it overlooked a garden. I imagined us warming up before the show. Flowers in the dressing room. The two of us taking center stage in Kyoto. Surely this experience would only bring us closer together.

Tchaikovsky's music for the grand pas de deux of the Sugar Plum Fairy and her cavalier is grave and solemn. It's my favorite music in the ballet. As the music builds in intensity, the strings and horns compete in alternating spirals of highs and lows, as if yearning and acquiescing at the same time. Even filtered through the tinny speakers of the ballet studio, it sounds regal and sends shivers down my spine.

In Matt's version, the dancers walk toward each other from opposite sides of the stage on the harp's opening arpeggios. The cavalier offers his hand, and the Sugar Plum Fairy takes it as she extends her leg for a partnered balance.

In the outside world, "balance" is thought of as equilibrium, like the scales of justice or two parts of an equation—in other words, static. In ballet, balance is dynamic, resounding like an echo. Energy radiates through limbs in equal measure with total calm in the center. The illusion is the dancers are completely still. The reality is they never stop evolving.

When a dancer is already balancing on her leg, her partner's job is to keep her there. When she's not, it's his job to find it. From my first piqué arabesque to the last flurry of pirouettes, Matt knew just how much pressure to apply to keep me on my toes.

There was always an adjustment when dancing with a new partner, but Matt and I fit together like two halves of a whole. We shouldn't have been surprised, given the time we'd spent together, but we were experienced enough as dancers to know this onstage chemistry was rare.

"Let's do a helicopter on the big crash!" he said. "I never get to do that lift with my students."

The helicopter is more of a throw than a lift. The ballerina runs toward her partner. He throws her into the air over his head like a human whirligig, then catches her in a pose called a "fish." Executed correctly, a helicopter looks like the ballerina is caught seconds before her face would hit the ground. Technically speaking, it isn't a difficult lift, but it only works when both partners share the same sense of timing.

"I've never been able to do the helicopter," I said.

"You've just never had the right partner."

My last partner had always been quick to point fingers and skirt responsibility, then quick to take credit. Matt was different. The helicopter lift worked the first time we tried it. And the second. And the third. Would we be able to repeat it in the performance? That would be the real test.

But if I thought about the climax—if the lift would work or if the balance would echo—if I concentrated on "later" instead of "now," I'd miss everything.

The beauty of ballet—the pleasure of dancing—happens in the present. That's not a metaphor. That's the reality of dance.

Matt started the CD for our final run-through, and as I walked toward him, I realized how our rehearsal was like a mirror of our relationship. If I focused on how the "later" part would manifest, I would miss the "now" of it. And maybe the space between phone calls wasn't dead air. Maybe it was just the time we needed to catch our breath between dramatic lifts—time I could use to find my ballerina balance in the outside world as I memorized JavaScript syntax and revised essays for my college applications. I didn't need to ask what we were doing. We were perfectly matched, and we were enjoying the dance. I knew this with as much certainty as I knew that Matt would catch me in a perfect fish after the helicopter.

Ten days before we were supposed to leave, I got a voicemail. Vandals, possibly Russian mafia, had broken into the ballet studio in Kyoto and destroyed everything—mirrors, barres, scenery. There would be no *Nutcracker.* It was a ridiculous claim, but this much was clear: Matt and I were not going to dance the Sugar Plum pas de deux in Japan.

"Of course the gig was going to fall through," Matt said when we met for dinner that night. He marked off red flags on his fingers. "The contract that got 'lost in the mail.' Flight details that were 'almost finalized.' They probably found someone cheaper to dance. Someone local."

He popped an unagi roll into his mouth. I picked at my wakame salad.

"You knew?" I asked. "Why didn't you say anything?"

"Well . . ." Matt chewed slowly, as if choosing his words carefully. "Our rehearsals were performance-perfect. But only because we were fully committed. We wouldn't have tried as hard if we thought it wasn't real."

I considered this and its subtext. I was still disappointed. "Yeah, but I really wanted to dance together."

"We did dance together! And trust me, we'll have lots more

chances. I'm sure of it. I'm not going anywhere. Are you?"
I shook my head. He offered his hand, and I took it.

One morning I woke up only to discover that I couldn't get out of bed. My body had had enough.

My on-the-job injury had entitled me to several months of physical therapy. There were weekly appointments with an osteopath and daily yoga classes. Three times a week I visited a sports clinic for a carefully prescribed combination of sports massage, ultrasound therapy, and Pilates exercises. Each session lasted three hours.

On a good day, I could walk to the bus stop without limping. I could sit down for an hour or more without my psoas muscle cramping. On a normal day, the special exercises from my physical therapist made sitting in a chair tolerable as I banged out code for web pages and polished my résumé for dotcom jobs. But on a bad day I stood, clutching whatever I could find—a pole, a railing, the back of a barstool—until the spasms subsided and the pain receded.

At night in bed after a cocktail of wine, ibuprofen, and a heating pad, I scrolled through my victories in my mind's eye: that time at the Kennedy Center where I kneeled downstage with the front leg perfectly turned out; a sublime sauté arabesque in the amphitheater at Il Vittoriale degli Italiani; the lullaby solo in *The Firebird* at McKelligon Canyon, when my entire family was in attendance. Like a film in slow motion, I freeze-framed each moment, reinforcing the memories. There was a plié on the count of four—just as the woodwinds sang—a relevé on five. Turning on six, seven, eight. Land. No wobbling. Flawless.

Not all scenes were performances. One of my top-five career-best moments was an à la seconde balance on tile floor when Sofia asked me to dance for her preschool class. My limbs sang like a high-C vibrato. Other scenes didn't even have an audience. Like that rond de jambe at the barre in Reggio Emilia in 1995. My left shoulder blade was flat reaching down through my spine, a counterforce as the right leg drifted in an exquisite arc from front to side to back.

That was a good rond de jambe.

I tried to remember what it felt like to be absorbed in each role without the fear of my ligaments catching and restraining my movement. Somewhere in the marrow of my bones, the emotions still flowed: the passion of a princess leaning toward her lover, the despair of a swan with a broken wing, the confidence of a mythical creature with the power to banish demons. Each character lived on like an epic poem, an oral history that would be forgotten unless I recited each stanza every night.

BEHIND THE SCENES

ON A WARM DECEMBER DAY, OUR COZY FAMILY OF THREE—DADDY, Mama, and daughter—headed from our home in Oakland, California, to a town called King City so Matt could perform his signature role as the Sugar Plum Fairy Cavalier. It would be our last road trip before the twins would be born, and Chiara had told me in her three-year-old way she was not pleased about this pregnancy. She wanted a sister, not two brothers. She couldn't understand why I wouldn't make what was growing inside me be something else.

Here's what she didn't know: These twins were monoamniotic/monochorionic. They shared a placenta and an amniotic sac, and doctors estimated I had fifty-fifty odds of getting through the pregnancy without major complications. The twins were not due until mid-April, but to be on the safe side, my doctor had scheduled a C-section in mid-February. It was the safest way. The risks for preemies who were born at thirty-two weeks could be mitigated by technology, the doctor insisted, while risks of them strangling themselves on each other's umbilical cords could not.

Here's what I didn't know: Every person who passed by and said, "Whoa! Looks like you're going to have a baby in a couple of weeks!" would be right. Two weeks later, at twenty-five weeks and four days, I'd go into labor. The boys would be born at the end of December, fifteen weeks before their April due date. They'd spend three months in the hospital. If we had known, Matt certainly wouldn't have taken this last-minute invitation to dance in King City, an unexpected and welcomed opportunity for one more set of *Nutcracker* performances.

Last year I spent my days translating code from one programming language to another, but during this pregnancy just eating balanced meals and taking naps was a full-time job.

"Mama, tell me a story!" our daughter demanded from the back seat.

Chiara had attended *Nutcracker* rehearsals with Matt since before she could crawl, but just this year it had clicked for her. Those people onstage were telling a story. And it's one she could relate to: a little girl gets a doll for Christmas.

"It is winter in Germany," I began. "It's so cold outside the milk bottles on the front steps freeze. Clara and Fritz are waiting for their cousins to come to their party."

My story was a mishmash of the *Nutcracker* versions I'd danced during my career, and many details were cribbed from the stories Ms. Heuser would tell us. The little girl who got the nutcracker was named Clara, not Marie. Drosselmeier was kind and eccentric, not creepy and manipulative. The Mouse King had one head, not seven the way he did in the original fairy tale. When the battle was over, the nutcracker came to life and took Clara on a journey through the snow. The gist was this: Clara got a nutcracker, and because she defended him, she went to a magic fairyland.

King City, which was just a dot on the map off Highway 101, had one motor inn, and that's where the King City Ballet Academy had put us up for two nights to cover one dress rehearsal and two performances. The theater was six blocks into town at the high school, across the street from the town's laundromat, grocery store, and taquería.

Traveling to a new city to dance for complete strangers was my favorite way to perform. It meant that my relationship to the audience was purely based on my dancing, not who I was outside of dance. This emphasized the phenomenon I love most about the performing arts. A ballet is simultaneously a process and a product, occurring in real time.

Other forms of art—painting, books, movies—exist in the world as physical things. A ballet, on the other hand, is tangible but not material. Sort of the same way a dream is remembered as concrete but experienced as fleeting. Before the curtain rises, the ballet doesn't even exist. It's just pieces: costumes, dancers, choreography. There's a musical score, sets, scenery, props, light cues. But none of it by itself is the ballet until it is danced for an audience.

After the curtain falls and the dancers have taken their final bows, the performance becomes a shared memory that means something different to each participant, from Fritz to the Sugar Plum Fairy Cavalier. From a three-year-old watching Daddy dance for the tenth time to a wife remembering her own career. We experience the ballet together but hold the memory in a way that is uniquely ours.

This is why audiences could return to *The Nutcracker* year after year. This is how I could dance it fifty times in a single month, and it would still feel fresh. Each show exists in the moment it is performed and then only exists once, even if the piece is repeated a thousand times.

This is why a performance feels like magic.

My husband's approach to ballet was less philosophical. He liked the physicality of it. Each iteration was an opportunity to improve on his technique and execution. That's how he stayed motivated for hundreds of rehearsals and annual performances. Perhaps it mirrored his tenure as a basketball player in high school before he discovered dance in college.

The clerk checked us in, and she brightened when she read Matt's name. "You're the star dancer! I'm going to see you tomorrow. Got my tickets and everything. My granddaughter's dancing. My husband is helping out backstage. You know, we used to have a *Nutcracker* every year. Then about twenty years ago the director went to Europe. We're pleased as punch that she's back." She handed us two keys and a handful of meal vouchers for the motor inn's restaurant.

In our room overlooking the highway, I unpacked our suitcases, separating dance clothes from day clothes. It felt like a preperformance ritual, although with books, toys, and prenatal protein shakes, there was more to unpack than just dance accoutrements.

The Robert Stanton Theater, the high school auditorium where the King City Ballet Academy performed, was a full-sized theater. It was enormous for any high school, let alone one in a town that boasted of only one stoplight. It had a balcony and a full light board, which meant there were two spotlights in the balcony and four light trees backstage. It had been built in 1939 as part of the Works Progress Administration and Federal Arts Project, two New Deal agencies that provided jobs during the Great Depression. The theater was listed on the National Register of Historical

Places. Many of the external decorations looked similar to the Grand Opera House in Uvalde, Texas, where I danced when Ballet El Paso took its production of *The Nutcracker* on tour the year the bus got a flat tire.

"We are so glad to meet you!" The director of the King City Ballet Academy smiled broadly as she shook Matt's hand. She nodded at me. "This is our first *Nutcracker* in many years. We've had just twelve weeks to get things up and running again. Let me give you a tour around." She looked at Chiara. "Are you here to see Daddy dance?"

No one would have ever pegged me as a former professional ballet dancer, especially in my current condition five months pregnant with twins. I liked the anonymity. Part of me liked to give Matt center stage, but mostly, it embarrassed me to talk about my career.

On paper it looked impressive: training on scholarship at San Francisco Ballet, Pacific Northwest Ballet, and in Ghent, Belgium, and dancing in Europe before coming back to San Francisco.

The truth of it was that my career felt like a patchwork quilt. My notable roles were in obscure ballets with small dance troupes. My few stints with A-list companies were spent in the corps de ballet. Not all the work was steady, and during the dry spells, I'd return to El Paso to dance for Ms. Heuser.

Upon reflection, the whole of my ballet career was smaller than the sum of its jobs.

While I was dancing, I loved what I did. The big companies provided security while the small ones offered eclectic opportunities, such as performing in a medieval castle or in an amphitheater nestled in the mountains. And dancing in El Paso gave me a chance to save money and spend time with family.

But just when I felt as if I had it all figured out—how to be artistically fulfilled and financially solvent—I had fallen. By the time I'd finished with physical therapy, the idea of auditioning to find new work was exhausting. It made more sense to find a new line of work—such as writing code for websites. Matt was there to support me through a career transition from ballet to software, and I've supported his careful balance of an office day job and ballet gigs. These days I'm content to skirt the spotlight and play a supporting role as wife and mother.

"This is probably so much smaller than what you're used to," the director said, gesturing to the stage.

"It's beautiful," Matt said. "I can't believe this is a high school auditorium."

She nodded proudly. "We make do. Dressing rooms are in the back. You're on stage left. I think you've got about an hour before we'll start on Act II. Please make yourself at home."

Matt gave a little stage bow, and the director returned to the rehearsal in progress. It had been many years since I'd danced in this ballet, but I could still hear Ms. Heuser's voice. In King City, she would have criticized the choice of wearing white at a Christmas party, and she would have yelled at the dancers for moving their lips during their pantomime.

Too tiny to see over the seat in front of her, Chiara tried to get comfortable on my lap. There wasn't much room for her to sit. My belly took up most of the space that used to be all hers.

Why does Drosselmeier have an eye patch? she wanted to know, only the way she said it, it came out as "Why dud de haf da eye patch?"

Good question. I'd never thought about that. Why did Drosselmeier have an eye patch? The real answer was that Drosselmeier had an eye patch to make the audience uneasy. Could this guy be trusted or not?

I gave Chiara the preschool-appropriate answer.

"Because he's mysterious."

"What's so mysterious about an eye patch?" she asked, which came out as "Why dat miteereyuss?"

Fair point. It was just an eye patch.

Next to us in the aisle, Matt stretched on the floor. His phone vibrated with a call from his sister.

"Hello?" he whispered as he quickly walked back to his dressing room.

Onstage, the party guests said their goodbyes. In the wings, Clara changed into her dressing gown, waiting for her next entrance, the transition from the party scene to the battle. Soon the tree would grow, and the mice would come to challenge Clara's nutcracker.

Drosselmeier crossed from stage left to stage right with his eye patch and equally mysterious cape. A stagehand sneaked behind a papier-mâché grandfather clock with owl wings on the sides of the clock's face. He shuffled to the front of the stage.

"Stop!" The director clapped her hands. "Fred? When you do that, can you make sure you are still really close to the wing? That way we don't see the little mice when they come out of the clock. Thanks."

Thanks? I tried to imagine Ms. Heuser thanking one of her stagehands for doing his job.

"Little mice? Are you ready backstage?" The director turned to the gaggle of seven-year-old girls sitting in the front row, clearly not ready for their entrance.

"My goodness! You're not backstage!" she scolded, but still in a friendly voice. "It's almost time for you to come out! Go! Go! Take your places."

The stage was lit, and the house was dark. The director

shielded her eyes and looked toward the sound booth. "Alejandro? Can you take it from Drosselmeier's crossing?"

Alejandro started the music again. Drosselmeier swept across the stage. Fred pushed the clock. The owl wings flapped as the prop struck midnight.

Chiara counted along. "One! Two! Four! Seven! Thirty!"

One by one, little mice hopped out from behind the clock and circled around Clara as she cradled her nutcracker.

"Mama, mice don't hop." Chiara shook her head. The little mice piqued her interest because they were the dancers closest in size to her own. She pointed at one who had forgotten her steps. "Dey not ve-wy good!" A bold statement for someone who herself wasn't coordinated enough to skip.

"It's hard to remember all those steps," I said, admitting to myself that not only would Ms. Heuser have agreed with her, she would have yelled at those little mice for "woo-ining her ballet."

Onstage, Clara walked slowly backward toward the audience as the tree grew. Or was she shrinking? Mice-shaped shadows flew over the stage. On the CD, the string section and the horns modulated in a musical spiral, a melody full of tension, excitement, and foreboding.

For me, no Clara would ever replace my memories of Dee Bee in her long nightgown with the laced cuffs and collar.

Of all the scenes she danced, she was at her most resplendent during the interlude in which Drosselmeier's magic makes the tree grow. Each night she'd circle the stage, sometimes with piqué turns, other times in a dramatic manèges of grand jetés. Dee Bee would often immerse herself so fully into a role she'd forget the steps. Only those of us familiar with the choreography knew when she was improvising. Everyone else saw only the fierce emotions she conveyed. She was a Clara simultaneously bewildered by the magic around her and determined to rise to the challenge. *I don't know what's happening, but I will stand up for the ones I love. I will defend my nutcracker.*

Through the loudspeakers, a cymbal crashed. Onstage, the Christmas lights on the fake tree sparkled to match the twinkling of percussion instruments.

Matt tiptoed down the center aisle toward our seats.

"I have to call my mom," he whispered. "Something's wrong with my dad."

From stage right, a soldier marched to center stage and fired a warning shot.

After we put Chiara to bed, we huddled in the bathroom of our motel room. In a hushed whisper, Matt filled me in on the details of the day's phone calls.

"My dad has a tumor in his abdomen. The doctor thinks it might be as big as fifteen pounds. It's possible that it's been growing for years. He'll have surgery. And if that doesn't work, chemotherapy or radiation."

The news sat there between us. A fifteen-pound tumor? It sounded impossible. Matt's dad was only sixty-eight. He competed in triathlons. Someone like that seemed too healthy to have cancer.

During the short months of my risky twin pregnancy, Matt and I had come to equate being informed with being prepared. Surely cancer was no different. We were certain that Wikipedia and Google could tell us everything we needed to know to be armchair oncologists. This was our last innocent moment, the last time in our lives when we harbored the naive optimism that a truckload of facts could predict an outcome.

In the coming months we would tackle each obstacle as it appeared.

Two weeks from now, when a routine ultrasound showed that I was in preterm labor, we would go to the hospital.

When the twins were born, hovering at a pound and a half apiece, we would call for reinforcements. My mother would come to stay with us.

Matt would get permission from his boss to work part-time from our apartment.

The twins would come home after a three-month stint in the hospital.

We would do the math. We could not live on a paralegal's salary, but we might be able to do it if Matt went to law school.

When Matt's father needed a second surgery, then a third, Matt would fly to Florida to be at his father's side.

As our twins became more robust, their grandfather's health would decline.

After the last finals of the spring semester of Matt's first year at law school, we would get the call.

When we went to the funeral, my mother would stay with our children.

Each task would be performed with technical efficiency, even grace. Like my career, our milestones would look like a seamless run of accomplishments. In reality, they had more in common with Dee Bee's improvisation. Sometimes we experienced the grief in real time. Other days we pushed it away the same way I'd ignored the pain of blood blisters on the knuckles of my toes.

The King City Ballet Academy version of *The Nutcracker* had a bit of a potluck feel to it. Many of the costumes looked as if they were brought from home—such as the white dress from the party scene—and the cast was small and very young. Matt and his partner were not just the only professionals, they were also the only dancers above the age of fifteen. Many dancers performed several roles, and Fred had to hold the curtain for a brief pause between the battle and the snow scene because most of the mice were also snowflakes. Still, it was a full-length production of *The Nutcracker* with two sold-out shows. And put together in just twelve weeks. That in itself was impressive.

While Matt alternated between offering hopeful texts to family members and warming up backstage, I tried one last time to convince Chiara to go to the bathroom before the show started.

"It's time to go potty!"

"I dohna need to go," she insisted, shaking her head.

Maybe she didn't, but I did. My belly was so heavy it bore down on my bladder. If I'd stopped for a moment to let my brain register what my body was telling it, I would have recognized this feeling. This was how I felt in the days just before Chiara was born.

In the foyer, mothers and aunts from the ballet school had set up concessions to sell. There were toy nutcracker ornaments, candy canes in felt reindeer sheaths, and chocolate chip cookies in Christmas-themed cellophane wrap.

"Would you like a cookie, little girl?" said a woman as she arranged poinsettias on the table. She gestured to the trays of Rice Krispies treats and candy canes next to the ballerinas made from pipe cleaners.

Chiara's eyes widened and she looked at me. She knew her best chance for treats was not directly asking for them. I nodded solemnly, and she shyly grinned as she selected a snack.

"What an adorable little girl! How old?"

"Three years old in February."

"And little brother or sister?" The woman pointed to my belly. "Expecting a Christmas baby?"

"Something like that," I said. I was just as reluctant to talk about our twin pregnancy as I was about my ballet career.

"You're the family that's come down to be the stars!" One of the fathers extended his hand for me to shake. Last night I saw him decorating Christmas trees in the lobby. "You know, the last time King City had a *Nutcracker*, I danced in it!" He chuckled and patted his beer belly. "It was a long time ago."

The preshow buzz in the lobby was different from my experience as a dancer and spectator. No one here—not the ushers, not the parents—seemed to be in a hurry to watch the show. Instead, fathers who had laid down the Marley floor and mothers who had sewn sequins on tiaras stood around smiling and hugging as they congratulated each other on their collective success.

Finally, the director came to shoo everyone into the theater.

"Come on! Come on! It's time to start!"

When we found our seats, Chiara wiggled on top of my lap.

"No room!" she complained.

The lights lowered. From somewhere in his sound booth, Alejandro started the CD. And just like that, it was Christmas Eve onstage.

The party scene was a little lean and the scenery was sparse, but I knew from eavesdropping in the lobby that it had been finished in the garage of the same dad whose daughter danced the part of the Ballerina Doll, the Snow Queen, and Spanish Chocolate. I imagined he beamed with pride at his contribution.

This was what had been missing from my philosophy of the performing arts. I had always considered the roles of the collective sum of dancers, choreography, and sets, but I'd never considered the role of the community. Perhaps because in a small company like Ballet El Paso, criticism overshadowed volunteer enthusiasm, and in the big companies, the players were paid professionals.

I didn't know yet that a patchwork community would be our lifeline over the next two years—through the birth of our sons and the death of their grandfather. Not facts from the Internet.

Chiara squirmed in my lap as one of the twins gave my ribs a solid kick.

Onstage, little mice hopped around Clara. Drosselmeier crossed the stage one final time before the tree started to grow.

Between crashes of cymbals, the horns swirled, as if they were traipsing down a spiral staircase while the strings modulated higher and higher. Hope and uncertainty mingled before meeting together with another crash.

It is Clara's last innocent moment. She has no idea that soon she'll be caught in the crossfire between life-sized toy soldiers and giant mice wielding weapons. She will come to the aid of her nutcracker, though, and it will change everything.

LITTLE ANGELS

WHEN I BRIBED MY TODDLER WITH CHEESE TO MAKE HIM point his feet, I knew exactly what I was doing: fostering a love of dance by manipulating my son's fondness for dairy products. I'd hold up a cube of mild cheddar, and Wayne would point his feet. While he was distracted by his snack, I'd cup his doughy little toddler feet in my hands and gently push on the metatarsals to stretch his arches.

"Again cheese?" he'd ask, grinning. Clearly, I had picked the right incentive.

Of my three children, Wayne was best suited for such an experiment. Chiara had never needed such encouragement; she'd been shimmying to music since before she could crawl. John, Wayne's twin, tended to speak his mind and question authority— both undesirable qualities for dancers. By contrast, Wayne was easygoing and a little bit dreamy. I didn't know if he wanted to be a professional ballet dancer, but luck favors the prepared, as they say. And boy, did he love cheese.

Besides, I wasn't making him do anything he didn't want to do. I was just pointing him in the right direction, so to speak, like a bobsled driver running alongside the sled as it gets going.

The difference was that as a parent, I knew I would eventually have to let him go on without me.

Until that juncture—again, cheese.

When Wayne turned four, I decided it was time to give him a taste of the stage. We—I mean, *he*—auditioned for *The Nutcracker*. In spite of a shocking inability to remember choreography and an astounding lack of musicality, Wayne was cast as a little angel. I had my work cut out for me in our home rehearsals. Our makeshift stage was the living room, and it didn't occur to me that the baseball game on TV might be a distraction.

After I'd retired from ballet but before I had children, I turned to baseball and the San Francisco Giants to vicariously experience what I was no longer able to do with my own body. Going to the ballet had become unbearable. My muscles would involuntarily jerk with recognition as if I could still land a triple pirouette or kick the back of my head in sissonne attitude. And then my mind would recall the pang of a torqued knee or a spasm in the lumbar spine. The visceral sensations slammed together like a head-on collision, leaving me battered and embittered.

Baseball was all men. The swings and slides had no overlap with the motor patterns burned into my brain, leaving room for other neural pathways to light up. Every time a player stepped up to the plate, it triggered the memory of stepping onstage in a demanding role. The flutter of anticipation felt like applause.

This time we're going to nail it.

The satisfying crack of the bat, a splash hit, a slide into home. It was almost as gratifying as the time I landed that double en de dans into a relevé arabesque onstage as a mythical firebird.

Almost.

Even the failures had felt good. I had been more under-standing with the Giants than I had been with my younger dancer self. The dropped fly ball in right field. The missed tag. The third strike.

That's okay. We'll come back tomorrow and try it again.

It had felt like therapy . . . that is, if sessions lasted four hours and therapists charged $17.00 for a beer and garlic fries.

But now I watched the Giants only when they were in the playoffs, and this year they were in the World Series against the Kansas City Royals. I kept tabs on them in an offhand way—with a muted television in the background. I had more pressing concerns, such as getting Wayne to rehearse without the promise of cheese, which he would eventually have to give up if he were to turn professional.

"Arms up on the count of *four*," I reminded him for the eighteenth time in sixteen counts, only to find him frozen in mid-plié.

"What's that?" he asked, nodding toward the television.

"It's a baseball game," I replied in a monotone. "Those are the San Francisco Giants. But they aren't really giants. They're just called that."

I thought if I answered in a boring voice, we'd get back to the rehearsal in progress.

"Who's that?" Wayne walked slowly toward the TV like a zombie.

"That's the pitcher. Madison Bumgarner."

I waited for him to lose interest, but instead he swayed a bit from side to side, eyes wide. Jaw slack.

"Who's . . . who's *that*?"

"That guy is the catcher. Buster Posey. The pitcher is going to throw him the ball, and the guy in blue is going to try to hit it."

Madison Bumgarner took the mound, and as he turned his head toward home plate, Wayne copied him and turned his chin over his shoulder. Madison wound up and threw a clean strike, and Wayne's body twitched, as if something inside his bones recognized those moves.

Over the next forty-five minutes, I explained balls, strikes, slides into home, and what it meant when the ball went over the wall. I explained that Pablo Sandoval, the slugger they called "Kung Fu Panda," wasn't a real panda and the outfielder's name was "Hunter Pence," not "Underpants."

By the seventh-inning stretch, Wayne was completely absorbed in the game. He found an empty paper towel roll to be his bat and a fleece mitten to use as his baseball glove. He was even scratching his crotch. He was still wearing his ballet slippers, but only because they were useful for sliding into second base, which just an hour earlier had been a humble ficus plant near the fireplace.

It dawned on me that the whole time Wayne pointed his feet for cubes of cheese—he just did it for the cheese.

But so what? I could be a baseball mom just as easily as I could be a stage mother. My ad hoc knowledge of how to stretch quadriceps and hamstrings, my list of chiropractors who made house calls, and my stash of Italian clay that reduced swelling in sprained ankles wasn't just applicable to ballet. Maybe I could sign him up for T-ball after *The Nutcracker* shows were over.

One month after the Giants won the World Series, on dress rehearsal night, the Kung Fu Panda was traded to the Red Sox. I didn't tell Wayne—not right away. I didn't want anything to interfere with his concentration. Although I knew that if he hadn't learned by now that the little angels had to raise their arms on the count of four, he'd never learn.

When I broke the news, he burst into tears.

"Why, Panda, why?" he cried into his pillow.

I've had my share of heartbreak. Boys who didn't want me. Ballet companies that didn't want me. I'd even known baseball grief. I, too, had had a beloved third baseman traded to the Red Sox. But those collective miseries were nowhere near as crushing as bearing witness to the shattered heart of a four-year-old.

I always thought letting go would mean watching from the sidelines as my children soaked up well-deserved glory. It didn't occur to me that letting go would also mean watching helplessly as they suffered, sharing their pain yet unable to lessen the anguish. As long as they hurt, I would hurt.

I sat on Wayne's bed in silence and rubbed his back as he sobbed, hoping it still counted as comfort.

SPANISH

THE INVITATION CAME THROUGH FACEBOOK, FOLLOWED BY A flood of texts from dancers. Ms. Heuser was having a pool party, a reunion for anyone who had ever danced with her. Our family was visiting my mother in El Paso that summer, staying in the house I grew up in, and sleeping in the same bedroom where I'd done my nightly stretches as a teenager.

"I think you should go," Matt said.

"Why? So she can tell me how terrible I was?" I launched into my impersonation of Ingeborg.

I lumbered to the kitchen counter. Wearily perching myself on a barstool, I sighed loudly, as if I were trying to infect him with my breath, and threw my arms up in a motion I'd seen in the ballet studio a million times since I was a kid. "What are you *doing*?" I exclaimed in a raspy singsong voice, timing my final word with a slap of my thighs. "You woo-ined my ballet!"

It was Ms. Heuser who taught us how to imitate other people in the first place. She's the one who told us to study the hands and to wait two beats between facial expressions. Under her persistent tutelage, we learned to take the most obvious characteristic of someone's gait and exaggerate it. In a perverse way, it was to her credit that we could mock her so accurately.

"Dude, that's harsh." Matt shook his head. "All teachers are a little crazy. Who was that one friend of yours in Italy?" My friend Fulvio had impeccable double tour en l'airs (a step that involves jumping and rotating twice in the air before landing), but he learned them the hard way: his teacher made him practice in the corner. If he didn't jump straight up and down, he'd hit his head on the wall. Matt laughed at the recollection.

"Harsh? I'll tell you what's harsh. One year a dancer had a seizure during barre. She actually fainted. Ms. Heuser didn't even stop the class. She said, 'You look green,' and demonstrated the next combination. Sofia refused to keep dancing and stayed with the girl until the ambulance came while Ms. Heuser continued class as if nothing had happened."

"That was a long time ago. I'm sure she's different now."

I wasn't so sure. I'd returned to El Paso so many times hoping exactly that, only to be disappointed.

I had come back to dance in Ms. Heuser's *Nutcracker* during my Christmas break in Iceland. The contract was barely enough to pay for my round-trip ticket from Reykjavik, but the Icelandic Ballet had turned out to be a metaphorical freeze-out—for me, anyway. The director, an Icelandic woman newly retired from the Deutsche Oper Berlin, didn't like the dancers she'd inherited because they weren't classical enough. The dancers didn't like the director because after a lifelong career abroad, she wasn't Icelandic enough. The only thing they could agree upon was their mutual dislike of the ballet master who'd hired me. It was like being thrown into a family argument of a family that was not mine. I hadn't told anyone yet, but upon returning to Reykjavik after Christmas break, I had planned to follow up with some Italian friends and try my luck dancing in Italy.

That Christmas I returned home like the prodigal son. And

like the father in the Bible story, Ms. Heuser welcomed me with open arms. She cast me for several roles in *The Nutcracker*, including my signature role as Fritz. It was just the boost I needed to keep dancing.

At first, Italy wasn't the Promised Land either. I didn't have a work permit, and while some companies were willing to pay me under the table, they were also the sort of companies with reputations for not compensating their dancers at all. My other job offer came from a director notorious for his preference for dancers who'd compromise their virtue in exchange for the promise of roles. Again, El Paso looked good by comparison. At least I'd have *The Nutcracker*.

When I came home for Christmas the following year, I gave Ms. Heuser a call. But this time, it was not the blessed homecoming from the Bible stories.

"Do you think I need you to come in and save the day?" she snarled. "I have plenty of dancers, and they don't come and go as they please."

On opening night, I sat in my father's living room, and I opened a bottle of wine I'd brought with me from Verona. We looked at the clock. Right now at the theater, Ms. Heuser would be pinning wigs and yelling at stagehands. I had never spent Christmas in El Paso and *not* danced in *The Nutcracker*.

I was debating a second glass of wine when the phone rang. It was the mother of one of the dancers.

"Christina left. Ms. Heuser might need you to take her place in 'Spanish Chocolate.'"

I was in the middle of trying to figure out what to say when the call-waiting beeped. It was Ms. Heuser. She was frantic. I could hear the music of the "Grandfather's Dance" in the background. The party scene was almost over.

"I need you to dance!" she said breathlessly.

If I hadn't been forewarned, I would have thought it was Sofia calling to play a prank. I grabbed my dance bag and my makeup kit, still unpacked from Italy, and drove to the theater.

Reports varied. Some people said that Christina's back had been seizing up all week. Her chiropractor advised against performing, but Ms. Heuser wouldn't listen. Others said that Christina had planned to put her in the lurch all along. She'd taken the warm-up in full makeup and then as soon as it was over, grabbed her bag and snuck out the back.

At first no one said anything. They just assumed she was taking a cigarette break. By the time the overture started, it was obvious she wasn't in her dress for the party scene. By then, it was too late to say anything—everyone had to go onstage themselves. When Ms. Heuser realized what had happened, she was in the audience. She called me from the pay phone in the foyer.

I had just enough time to get dressed.

The other dancer in the Spanish variation—a woman I'd never met before—eyed me warily. "Are you sure you know what you're doing?"

"Don't worry," I tried to reassure her. "I know everything but the finale, and we can go over that later."

Onstage adrenaline and muscle memory took over. I felt like sunshine.

After the show, we were all invited to the opening-night party at the board president's house. I usually hated going to the opening-night parties. The good food was always gone before I'd changed and packed out of the theater, and I viewed the compliments strangers gave me with suspicion. I was always sure they didn't really remember which part I'd danced. Or that their effusive praise was faked or obligatory. But this time, I knew I'd saved the show. I wasn't about to miss my victory lap.

Ms. Heuser never said a word to me. At the party, her gaze floated over me as if I were invisible.

I vowed never to come back. When my paperwork was finally approved by the Italian consulate, I returned to Italy. Work was patchy but rewarding. I danced in a medieval castle and in elaborate theaters. I performed on Belvedere overlooking Florence and in Piazza Barberini in Rome. There was never enough work and never enough money. I would have gone back to El Paso every year if I could have been sure Ms. Heuser would have valued me.

"That was so long ago," Matt said. "She wouldn't have a reunion if she didn't want to see you."

I called Sofia. "I'll go if you go."

"I don't want to go. You're the only person I'd want to see anyway."

"That settles it," I said. "Let's have our own reunion."

"Ardovino's at seven," she said.

We met at an Italian restaurant across from The Ballet Centre, one of Ms. Heuser's first ballet studios. When we were kids, we practiced walkovers for "Mother Ginger" in that studio.

"What kept us dancing? Did we ever know we were good?"

Sofia sipped her wine. "Did I ever tell you that she came to see me dance in *Peter Pan*? It was the dinner theater. And afterward she went backstage and told me, 'You were amazing!'" Sofia widened her eyes and continued in her best Ingeborg voice. "'You could have gone to New York!' And I thought, *All those years I danced for you. That's all you had to say. Just once.*"

I was stunned. Not just that Ms. Heuser had given such effusive praise but also, how did Sofia not know that she had been an amazing dancer? What would it have taken for any of us to know that?

ARABIAN

MATT STOOD ONSTAGE IN HIS ARABIAN COSTUME NEXT TO the Arabian princess, a young dancer who would graduate from high school in the spring. I was huddled in the back of the theater, taking notes. This budding ballerina wasn't quite sure how to keep her body compact, but Matt was strong enough to compensate for her inexperience. All season they had been working on the arabesque presságe that happened on center stage on the fading notes of the pas de deux. Sometimes it worked. Often it didn't. This was not something Matt could fix with brute strength. This was a combination of timing, coordination, and cooperation. If they couldn't make it work tonight, the director would take it out.

If this were one of his stronger partners, such as the girl he would partner on Sunday for the Sugar Plum pas de deux, he would have rolled through his repertoire of jokes. When the snowflakes fell from above, he'd say, "Hey—is that asbestos?" or "Remember the new ending!" when he and his partner were just about to run onstage. He was like the backstage class clown. Unless, like now, there was a lift on the line.

Ever since Matt started his new job at a Silicon Valley law firm, rehearsing for *The Nutcracker* was one of the few things we did together as a family. It was forty miles from Oakland to Mountain View. On weekends, we'd wake up early to drive to the ballet studio. We'd arrive armed with apple slices and baby carrots for snacks and quesadillas for lunch. The twins' rehearsal was early in the morning before their ballet class, while Chiara's was in the afternoon. Some Saturdays I taught the older girls, the ones who were flowers and snowflakes. Other times I drilled the little angels or the Mother Ginger children. Meanwhile, Matt reviewed the pas de deux choreography with the high school seniors.

Before kids, we thought nothing of driving an hour south to San Jose, crossing a bridge north to Marin, or driving east through the tunnel to Walnut Creek to be in a show. We went wherever the gig was. Every dancer did that.

Even after kids, it was manageable at first. Matt took Chiara to rehearsals with him. There was always a mother or older dancer eager to play with her while Daddy danced. Through his three years of law school, he scheduled classes and study time around *Nutcracker* obligations. But now, we were at a breaking point. He'd leave for work before the kids awoke, and return late at night after they were in bed. Sometimes days passed when they didn't see Daddy at all. I was glad these last *Nutcracker* rehearsals meant that soon we'd get back to normalcy.

The director spoke into the microphone, and the music stopped.

"You need to cover equal territory from opposite sides of the stage for the presságe to work," she said. "You need to bourrée on a sharper diagonal. And Matt, you need to take fewer steps."

Brightly colored strips of tape dotted the floor to divide the stage in halves, quarters, and eighths. Matt showed his partner which mark she needed to aim for.

"Let's try the lift one more time without music. Take it from the bourrées. Five-and-uh, six-and-uh, se-ven, and go!"

But just before she stepped into the arabesque, the Arabian princess hesitated, throwing the timing off. Matt saved the lift, but it looked as though he were bench-pressing dead weight. If the music had been playing, they would have missed their cue.

"Okay. Let's take it out. Do a piqué arabesque instead. Matt, take her at the waist and then just run off. Exit stage left."

The ballerina looked relieved—the piqué arabesque was a sure thing—but I could tell Matt was disappointed. I knew he'd been thinking that if they kept at it, they'd get the timing. He was right. Practice made perfect . . . eventually. But this Arabian princess was also a Dew Drop Fairy and a Snow Queen. She had other roles to concentrate on. At a certain point, it made sense to stop striving for the ideal and just take what was within reach.

At home, Matt sifted through the clean laundry I'd folded. "Yeesh. These tights sure have seen better days," he said as he pulled out his performance tights. "I will definitely need to get a new pair for next year."

Next year?

We hadn't explicitly discussed this would be his last *Nutcracker*. I didn't think we needed to. In the past, he never had to choose work over ballet or ballet over family. He'd been able to do it all. But soon law firm life would take precedence over everything. He'd known that since his paralegal days. It was part of the reason he'd waited so long to go to law school.

"Honey," I said softly, but not unkindly. "There is no next year. We can't keep doing this anymore. This is your last *Nutcracker*."

His stunned and hurt look was oddly satisfying to me.

"Don't you think I should get to decide when I quit?"

"Not when the whole family has to sacrifice for it." This was an unfair blow on my part. Matt put breakfast on the table before he left for work. He made every lunch. *The Nutcracker* season was not as long and demanding as it used to be. If we wanted to make it work, we could.

But I didn't want to make it work. I wanted him to get on with his life. His demanding job meant I was the one who got the children ready for school, soccer, ballet, and bed. I was the one who rearranged my schedule to drive kids to the doctor, dentist, and everywhere else they needed to go. His job was so demanding it dictated what kind of job I could have. I worked for a literary festival by designing and maintaining their website and author database. It was just a handful of hours a week, and I was lucky this was even an option. I was the one who made sacrifices. I was the one with limited choices. And he thought he was going to dance another year of *Nutcracker*?

"It's not like I'm really dancing. I'm just partnering. They need me," he argued.

"We need you!" I exclaimed. "And if you have to put in a lawyer's hours at the firm, when are you going to have time to rehearse? What time will be left over for us? You don't spend enough time at home as it is."

"I never complain that you don't spend enough time with the family," he countered.

"That's because all my time is family time!"

"Well! It's not an apples-to-apples comparison."

"Yeah. Because one of us is home all the time and one of us is never home."

Matt scowled and stuffed his tights into his bag. "I'm late," he said. And stormed out.

Early in our relationship, Matt asked if I liked to hike.

"Hikes are pointless," I had told him, which I wouldn't have said had I known his fondness for them. He'd research a trail, plan snacks and refreshments to coincide with lookout points, and scope out a restaurant for afterward. Later he'd take his kids—our kids—on hikes he'd name "Early Morning Fun Hike" and "The Hike of Hidden Delights."

But to me a hike was when you drove someplace, walked around, and then walked back to your car and drove home. If I was going to put one foot in front of the other, it would be heel forward, toes back, spiraling at the knee, collarbones lengthening, and chin raised. It would be for a greater purpose, like a pirouette or a pas de cheval. It wouldn't be just to *walk* on a dirt path. An errant rock could turn an ankle. Thick-soled shoes would make my calves tight. Carrying a backpack would stress my lower back.

"When you put it that way, it sounds stupid," Matt said. "Sometimes it's fun to just enjoy the view."

That didn't resonate with me either. I'd seen my share of pretty views. In Reykjavik, I would walk to the ballet studio from my apartment near City Hall. The street signs were in Icelandic, of course, and because daily snowdrifts changed the terrain, I could never figure out where I was—smartphones would not be invented for another two decades—but as long as I kept the majestic Mount Esja within my sights, I knew I'd find my way eventually. Stark white and perfectly triangular with Gulf Stream waters swirling at its feet, Mount Esja stood like an ancient mountain king. It was so incongruous to see snow juxtaposed with ocean, and it always made me feel hopeful. Two things I never imagined could sit side by side were there in nature. It was like a sign from the universe that nothing was too impossible to achieve.

But "fun"? No. I did not feel called to admire the view for funsies.

"Okay," Matt said. "Not a hike. There's something I've been wanting to do, but I can't find the right person to come with me. Do you know the seawall at Aquatic Park? I want to climb it." He had a glow of anticipation in his eyes, as if he had a list of romantic things to try on a date, and this was one of them.

Climbing a seawall seemed almost as pointless as taking a hike. But I wanted to be the right person, the person to say, "Yes." And who knew? Maybe it would be more exciting than it sounded.

We drove to a stretch of land nestled between Fisherman's Wharf and the Presidio. It was curved like the crook of an arm.

I'd been there many times, as a summer student at San Francisco Ballet eating forbidden Ghirardelli chocolate and later as a professional dancer performing at the Cowell Theatre at Fort Mason. It had never occurred to me to cross over the boundary of rocks that protected the shore from the waves of the bay.

"Are you sure we're allowed to do this?" I asked as we straddled the fat, rusted chain that separated the sidewalk from the water.

"Oh no. I'm pretty sure it's illegal. That's why I can't find anyone to come with me. Those currents are pretty wild. And the water's freezing. The last thing the Coast Guard wants is to fish idiots out of the bay."

"You mean idiots like us?"

"Oh no. We're dancers. We're not going to fall."

I looked down at the lumps of brown, porous boulders. They looked fake, like stage rocks, as if they were light enough to hurl across the bay. Aggressive waves lapped at them and receded between the cracks, leaving white sea-foam across the surface.

He extended his hand. "Come on. It'll be fun."

Twenty minutes later, we'd traversed twelve feet along the seawall.

"Isn't this fun?" His grin was genuine.

I shook my head.

"Look!" He gestured to the fog rolling in under the Golden Gate Bridge. His arm swept along the bright blue water. White sailboats dotted the bay, circling Alcatraz Island. Six years later, we'd have a wedding reception at the Aquatic Museum on the other side of this same wall.

I pointed to the tourists walking past, just a few feet away. "It's the same view from the other side of the chain."

He shook his head. "This is different. We earned it."

I wanted to be the kind of person who enjoyed the view and said, "This is good. This is enough." But I was not. I was afraid the moment I decided life was good, I'd stop trying for something better.

On opening night in Mountain View, I scrunched down in my seat in the last row of the balcony and closed my eyes. The more time passed, the more I worried that the memories embedded in my muscles would fade. But Tchaikovsky's music always coaxed them to the surface.

When the overture began, the quiet slash of strings took me back to El Paso: Mike Spence's announcements calling us to the stage from mustard-yellow dressing rooms; Mr. Chavez's baton nodding at the orchestra; and Dee Bee and I, standing in the wings, holding our breath, imagining we are locked in the dark closet of our German grandmother's house.

In Ms. Heuser's version, the parents danced offstage midway through the party scene, ostensibly to dine in some other room of the house. Only the children remained onstage. Watching Dee Bee dance with her doll, I'd seethe and scheme with the other boys. Dee Bee would offer her nutcracker to Sofia in a spirit of Christmas generosity, and that's when I'd seize my moment. I'd tear through the living room in gallops and leaps, intercept the toy at the handoff, and yank off its head. The audience would gasp and I'd soak it up. "Oh, I'm sorry. Did I break your nutcracker?"

Night after night, I'd grab it and smash it, even though I didn't really care about that stupid nutcracker. I just didn't want Dee Bee to have it.

Meanwhile, in Mountain View, it was the same music in the same order telling the same story. Party children skipped. Soldiers marched and mice scampered. Little angels raised their arms on the count of four . . . most of them, anyway.

The sultry music of the Arabian variation piped through the speakers in the auditorium. Cloying oboes and persistent bassoons coaxed and pleaded in a relentless pulse. I opened my eyes to watch Matt. From my vantage point, I saw the modifications he needed to make to keep his partner on her leg, and he did so effortlessly.

He really was good at what he did. That's why his dance career had lasted a full ten years longer than mine. There were never enough men in ballet. Consequently, there were never enough men who could partner well, even fewer who were willing to come for extra rehearsals, and an even smaller subset who already knew the choreography. As long as he could lift a partner and fit into the costume, this ballet studio would invite him to dance. There would never be a reality in which I got to be the breadwinner and Matt was relegated to chauffeur or in which I got to dance and he didn't. I was as envious sitting in the audience as I had been onstage as Fritz. And yet, every day of my career had felt like a struggle. Dramatic lifts were downgraded to piqué arabesques. There was always a shortage of pointe shoes. I barely made enough money to make ends meet. The cons always outweighed the pros.

So why do I wish I'd had more time?

Matt promenaded the Arabian princess in a circle as the clarinets whined. In lieu of an overhead lift, they ran offstage, exiting stage left, drawing out the last moans of the oboes.

CHINESE

WHEN JULY CAME AND WENT AND THERE WAS NO AUDITION
notice from Chiara's ballet school, no Doodle poll to survey my
rehearsal availability, and no newsletter from ballet companies
offering subscriber discounts, I knew. The Year 2020 would be a
Year Without a *Nutcracker*.

At first, I was relieved. I had spent the last four decades
immersed in *The Nutcracker*. First there were the years in the
audience. Then there were the years onstage. *The Nutcracker*
season still runs from September to December for me, but now
I spend it in the rehearsal studio teaching steps to the next
generation. I'd be lying if I said I never get tired of it. Every
year I get tired of it.

But that's not why I was happy for a reprieve from visions of
sugar plums. As a rehearsal assistant, I taught seven-year-olds to
dip and bow and shuffle on the correct counts to prepare them
for their fifty-eight seconds onstage in the "Chinese Tea" variation. On performance day, they donned black tunics with frog
buttons and Mandarin collars, their faces shadowed under coolie
hats.

I guess a part of me always knew the steps I taught were at
best an embarrassing show of artistic ignorance, and at worst a

shameful display of racist cultural appropriation. But I kept doing my job. *After all*, I told myself, *it's not my choreography.* I was just teaching the same steps students had danced for decades. Besides, everyone else seemed to be fine with it. When those seven-year-olds shuffled onstage, the whole audience cooed, "Awwww!" But each year, I winced a little more. It was not just fifty-eight seconds. It was months of Saturday afternoons, year after year, reinforcing a cultural stereotype on young minds, and I was the one demonstrating it. And because I was too nervous to confront the director of the school and label these time-honored steps as cultural misrepresentation (I mean, who did I think I was?), it was a relief to know that worries over COVID-19 contagion gave me a graceful out.

To be clear, by traditional *Nutcracker* standards, what I taught was not as offensive as the yellowface Fu Manchu mustaches and geisha wigs that appeared elsewhere. At Ballet El Paso, we wore actual pagodas on our heads. (I think Ms. Heuser was trying to mimic the *makuta* headdresses of Southeast Asia.) Many depictions were so racist and prevalent that an organization called Final Bow for Yellowface was founded in 2017 to confront these harmful Asian stereotypes in theater productions.

Their website offers a primer on how to respectfully honor and incorporate Chinese culture in *The Nutcracker*. Cultural appropriation is so rampant in *The Nutcracker* I can't imagine what the second act would look like without it.

When I was a student at Pacific Northwest Ballet in Seattle, I danced over 150 performances of a version of *The Nutcracker* that claimed authenticity by consulting the source, E. T. A. Hoffmann's *The Nutcracker and the Mouse King*. Maurice Sendak, who designed the sets and costumes, drew inspiration from the typical interior design of Bavarian aristocrats. The result was that the ballet was set against the backdrop of an eighteenth-century Ottoman seraglio dripping with Orientalism. In the Stowell/Sendak second act, Clara went to some exotic land, definitely the kind of place where wild things would be. Drosselmeier reemerged as a turbaned pasha. Clara and her prince were tended to by servants in fez-inspired caps and entertained by whirling dervishes in brownface, who wore nappy dreadlock wigs and dark brown unitards to simulate their bare-chested brawn. This wasn't 1950s nostalgia for racist minstrel shows. This was a production created in 1986 and performed up through 2014.

Standing in the wings getting ready for "Waltz of the Flowers" all those years ago, I didn't think anything of the black dreadlocks or dark brown makeup I saw onstage. At the time, it didn't seem any different from Ballet El Paso when my fellow Latina friends and I would whiten our skin with baby powder to "fit in" as snowflakes.

As an adult, I didn't know what was more disturbing to me—that there was once a time when I normalized whitening or darkening one's skin because I felt I wasn't enough of an artist on the inside unless I looked the part on the outside or that I didn't even notice the blatant racism around me. When I saw those brown unitards hanging up on the costume rack as a teenager, how did I not see it for what it was?

Even though the middle-aged me wouldn't say to her employer, "This 'Chinese Tea' variation is culturally inappropriate," I knew I had to demand better going forward. As a teacher, I could no longer be an accomplice to Spanish dancers with pseudo-flamenco steps, and Arabian princesses in sequined *I Dream of Jeannie* midriffs and harem pants. I couldn't condone rice paddy hats, even if they were worn by adorable seven-year-olds.

What's complicated was that the relief I felt from sidestepping the *Nutcracker* battle was still mingled with my own sentimental feelings toward the ballet. As if on cue, an internal timer chimed right around Thanksgiving, and I was surprised to find I felt a need for it, like an ache for comfort food. I missed teaching. I missed the miracle moments, such as when all twelve second graders realized that they needed to plié on the count of five to jump on the count of six—and they actually did it.

Nutcracker, I'll admit it—I can't quit you.

As every ballet dancer knows, *Nussknacker und Mausekönig* was written by E. T. A. Hoffmann in 1816, then retold by Alexandre Dumas père (the *Three Musketeers* guy)—and adapted by Tchaikovsky and his collaborators for the original Saint Petersburg ballet. Tchaikovsky's ballet spends the second act in the Land of the Sweets, where Clara (sometimes named Marie) watches an afternoon of dances supposedly from around the world, with official titles such as "Chocolate from Spain," "Coffee from Arabia," "Tea from China," and "Trepak." But in both Hoffmann's fairy tale and the Dumas version, there is no Land of the Sweets. No Spaniards. No consumer goods from Arabia or China. That international aspect was a convention of nineteenth-century balletomanes. It's not germane to the original text.

But what I didn't know until I turned to my local library's quarantine-friendly curbside pickup to soothe my sudden *Nutcracker* ache was that E. T. A. Hoffmann supplemented his writer's income as a civil servant in Prussia, where he earned a reputation as a judge who couldn't be bribed, even though this stance of moral integrity worked against him.

The Nutcracker and the Mouse King was a present to Hoffmann's godchildren, the real Marie and Fritz, who were the children of an upper-class ministry official. In it, Hoffmann nested life advice in a fairy tale that was in turn nested in a fairy tale.

The character Godfather Drosselmeier (arguably a stand-in for Hoffmann), who gifts the nutcracker to Marie in the first place, is the only adult who listens when Marie recounts her dreams. "The tree grew to an enormous size," she insists. She details a battle in which her nutcracker and his soldiers fight a mouse king with seven heads. The king is defeated when she throws her shoe at one of the crowns.

Everyone else tells Marie to keep her ideas to herself. Only Drosselmeier encourages her to break with social expectations, trust in her imagination, and quite literally, believe in her dreams.

Because she does this, Marie becomes the queen of a magic land "where you can see . . . the most splendid and wondrous things . . ." Hoffmann clarifies in his final lines, "if you have the right eyes to see them with."

I didn't know if I had the "right eyes" to have all the answers. But I did know that I missed the cacophony of instruments in the orchestra pit warming up on opening night and the magical moment when they became a single note before the overture began. I knew that when the conductor's baton lifted and paused, it was like the space before a breath or the centering of the soul. I knew Tchaikovsky's music, with its chimes and plucks and swirls, created a special kind of magic that tapped into a dancer's heart. I knew we were artists on the inside, regardless of what we looked like on the outside. And if we drew on that magic for new inspiration, we would create the most splendid and wondrous things.

RUSSIAN

EIGHT MIDDLE SCHOOLERS IN BLACK LEOTARDS AND PINK TIGHTS
sat on the floor of the ballet studio, waiting for rehearsal to start.
Instead of stretching or practicing, they chatted. One student
popped a cracker into her mouth and brushed the crumbs off her
fingers onto her tights. Another scrolled through her phone.

These *Nutcracker* rehearsals had little in common with those
from my youth. Because my teachers' stage had been reduced to a
ballet studio, they turned their rehearsals into a performance in
which they were the stars, and we were the captive audience. Oc-
casionally they'd turn the rehearsal into their own stand-up routine, but usually they held court by stomping around and hurling
insults. Some teachers blew smoke in our faces while we danced.
Others smacked us with canes. Then there were the endless
back-handed compliments.

"You look absolutely beautiful until you start to move."

"At least you aren't as fat as your mother."

In San Francisco, Mr. Gladstein kept order in a studio of sixty
dancers quite effectively when he paced menacingly back and
forth. In Seattle, Ms. Russell commanded respect and silence
simply by the way she carried herself. Would this be the day she
smiled and called you by name? Or would her gaze simply drift

over you? Insults were not the only way to make a person feel insignificant.

Mr. Howard, the ballet master who'd brought me to Reykjavik, scripted his snubs. "Are you bloated because you are on the pill, or are you drinking beer again?" And "You girls are the reason so many dancers are gay."

Ms. Heuser used a syrupy voice to tell young girls things like "Dahling, you look like a baby elephant when you jump." She saved her venomous tone for zingers such as "Suck in your stomach. You look like an Ethiopian child" or "You're so fat I bet you float."

She thought she was toughening us up by comparing our muscles to marshmallows and our feet to bricks. She believed it would make us try harder. All it did was sting us to the core, shake our confidence, and condone spitefulness between dancers. But I think she liked that effect. Ballet was supposed to be a fight. It was supposed to be cutthroat. Her verbal abuse kept us off-balance.

However, in North Oakland, ballet was supposed to be joyous. When my students left the studio, whether it was at the end of their schooling or just at the end of rehearsal, I wanted them to be inspired, not damaged.

The choreography I had to teach was simple. It mirrored the bouncy, upbeat music of the Russian Trepak, and even though practice lasted only thirty minutes every Saturday afternoon, it was more than enough time to learn the steps. My students were smart, and several had danced the variation before. By the middle of the first rehearsal, I'd taught most of the choreography. Still, I worried that I wouldn't have enough time. This was not like my childhood, where rehearsals ran long and dancers stayed until the director decided we'd danced well enough to be dismissed. Thirty minutes each week was all I got.

The problem wasn't the steps; it was the execution. The Russian variation was one of the most memorable melodies in *The Nutcracker*. It was bright and peppy, like the crack of a whip. The steps needed to be crisp and sharp, otherwise the whole dance sagged.

"You've got to snap the feet. Like this." I demonstrated a relevé passé. I flicked my foot to my knee, making a triangle shape between my toes and my thigh, not unlike tree pose in yoga class.

When I first started teaching in my twenties, I tried to reverse-engineer the mechanics of ballet. I corrected each detail as I saw it. *Move the heel forward. Toes back. Tummy in. Shoulders down. Backs long. Knees straight. Don't forget to point your feet!* I thought proper technique was learned through repetition, the way I learned to write cursive in grade school when I logged hour after hour at my desk, my cheek so close to the thin gray paper that it almost touched the blue dotted lines. I copied the same letters over and over until they had the right swoops and curves.

Unfortunately, rote practice was not enough to make ballet positions shimmer. The illusion of effortlessness was just as important as the aesthetic. Similarly, it wasn't enough to be graceful if you didn't hit the right landmarks as you moved.

Ballet was both a feeling and a shape, simultaneously a process and a goal. In any given moment, a dancer was both the eye of the hurricane and the turbulent winds. If my students could grasp these contradictory ideas and reach for the heavens while still acknowledging the pull of gravity, they would never falter. This was the difference between passé (dance) and tree pose (exercise). Well, that and the fact that yoga was an egalitarian philosophy unique to the individual. Ballet was beholden to its form.

The problem was, it didn't mean anything to tell someone they were both the eye and the storm. They still needed to be taught how to passé. The shoulders still needed to be down. The feet still needed to point.

"Your torso makes a box," I told my students. "Your shoulders and hips are parallel to the floor. When you plié, don't let the box tip. Now passé. Lift the toe, not the thigh. Make the foot snake up the leg like a vine growing up to the knee."

The dancers mimicked me but with lifted hips and tilted shoulders. They copied the shape but not the feeling. Relevé passé was a core step in the Russian variation. I tried again.

"You have to expand in five different directions. The knees bend, but behind the back of the ears you are lifting toward the catwalks up above. Your collarbones lengthen away from each other, like electric currents from your voice box through your fingertips. Your sternum projects to the audience."

This was supposed to be a light-bulb moment. My students stared blankly at me. I didn't know what was going on in their heads, but it was not the thrill of integrating artistry with technique. One student picked at a thread on her leotard. Another snuck a look at the clock.

This was when I should have made a noise loud enough to make everyone jump, to snap to attention, to get them to try a little harder. This was why my teachers used fear as a motivator. It was an effective way to get everyone on the same page.

Instead, I walked to the CD player. I wasn't a yeller.

"Let's take it from the top," I said, hoping the effervescence of the Trepak music might provide additional inspiration.

The students with an ear for music did the right steps on the right counts, while the ones with ballet sense had more precise shapes. But it was all perfunctory. They went through the motions because I'd told them to, as if this was how they'd chosen to pass the time on Saturday afternoons.

In my day, frustrated rehearsal directors would have stopped the run-through to tell stories of martyrdom from their own glory days. *If we had danced like that in rehearsal, our teachers would have caned us!* they might say. Or, in a move that was designed to inspire and intimidate at the same time, allusions to their brushes with fame: *If you only could have seen Gelsey/Sylvie/Alessandra/Natalia/ Yuan Yuan!* But I didn't want my students to find a connection to dance through my career. I wanted them to find it in themselves. Besides, our thirty minutes were up. Half my cast was already heading toward the door.

I didn't know what kept me dancing in spite of the negative reinforcement and the constant criticisms reminding me that whatever I did was never enough. From age seven to age thirty I danced to find out how I could be a better dancer. I performed to find my voice. Onstage, I tapped into something that was all mine, as if I had an inner light I could hold and shine at the same time. I could present it for everyone to see, but they couldn't touch it. The audience was just a witness. The dance was for me.

I didn't always find my inner light, but I always worked for it. When I did catch it, it felt like touching a live wire. There was the Gala performance in Reykjavik where I did a perfect triple piqué pirouette in front of a crowded house or the long arabesque balance as the Firebird at an amphitheater nestled in the mountains of West Texas. It wasn't always a technical achievement. One of my featured solos had a section where I simply walked downstage toward the audience. It was my favorite part of the dance. With each step, I felt myself glow brighter and brighter. Not all exquisite moments were solos either. When I could make my dancer's voice sing through my limbs, it was just as gratifying to be one of sixteen snowflakes.

At the last *Nutcracker* rehearsal, the pliés were not steady boxes. The passés still tipped over, and the relevés were still wobbly.

"And up! Up and up and up!" I repeated in a voice I liked to think of as "jaunty." I hoped my tone would convey the energy they needed to muster. At this late date, the most I could hope for was that my students enjoyed dancing their single performance.

At the end of rehearsal, I reviewed the logistics for the show: when to meet, what to bring, which electronics to leave at home.

"What are the three things I want you to do tonight?" I quizzed. The correct answers were limit screen time, eat a good dinner, and go to bed early.

One of the dancers raised her hand. "Take a shower!"

I sighed. "What are the *four* things I expect you to do tonight?"

In ten weeks of Saturday rehearsals, no one cried, there were no sprained knees from forced turnout, and no one fainted from unhealthy eating habits. We didn't even have any bloody toes, which, in itself, should have been a victory. I was hoping for something more, but perhaps it was just as important that they went home and bathed.

There was no barre in the cavernous room that counted as the dressing room. The space was shared with angels, battle soldiers, and Mother Ginger cookies. Despite constant reminders to quiet down, the dressing room buzzed with noise . . . but not nerves. No one was practicing steps or biting nails. They read books and played cards. I guessed it was a good sign no one was freaking out. But it didn't feel like the energy before a show. Did it mean we weren't prepared enough?

I led them in a short warm-up. At the start of the second act, they took their places in the wings, and I snuck into the audience to watch.

The opening trill of the Russian Trepak is like the striking of a match, and when it pulled the eight of them onstage, I was struck by their sameness. Not just because they had identical red coats and black hats. It was as if their enthusiasm vibrated on the same frequency. They were not nervous or embarrassed or hiding. It was like the laughter that only preteen girls can twitter—silly and formless and contagious. Just light and joy so bright it outshone the shape of their passés.

It was over as soon as it started.

The dancers ran offstage, breathless and effervescent. I met them in the dressing room.

"Oh my god, that was hella fun!"

"I could not stop smiling!"

They hugged and high-fived each other, and even though each one smiled at me in turn, it was clear—their exuberance was something I couldn't touch. Their joy was only something for me to witness.

NOT ALL SHEEP WHO
WANDER ARE LOST

THREE THOUSAND MILES AWAY, MY SIXTEEN-YEAR-OLD daughter texted me from the floor of her bathroom in the residence dorms. It was ten at night in Oakland. I should have been asleep already. It was one in the morning in Philadelphia. She, too, should have been asleep already.

I want to quit

The comment bubble was followed by three gray dots that pulsed and faded and pulsed and faded and pulsed and . . . stopped.

I didn't know the specifics behind tonight's text, but I suspected it was more of what she'd been repeating of late: Some of the girls in her class were younger and better. A few were much younger and much better, which compounded what she saw on social media, where everyone seemed to be much younger and much better.

Never mind that most of the dancers in her class were her age or older. Never mind that her name was engraved on a plaque at her home studio in recognition of her stage presence or that her nickname at her other summer intensive was "Balance Queen." I knew these observations were indisputable facts, but to repeat them only exacerbated her anxiety. Besides, one o'clock in the morning was not the time to make plans for the future or to engage in existential conversations around ballet and the life of an artist. I responded:

> I love you and I think you are a beautiful dancer. I also think that wanting to quit sounds like you are in the middle of a very intense summer! Can't wait to see you in 3 weeks. ;-)

She texted back.

> grrrr
> OK

I remembered that despair, the chasm between what I wanted to do with my body and what was reflected back to me in the mirror. I remembered the feeling that everyone else seemed to know something I didn't. Countless times, driving home from ballet, I'd sob in the car from whatever barbed bon mot Ms. Heuser had said to me in rehearsal that day.

Each time my mother would say, "Say the word and we are done. You never have to go back to that woman. You do not have to go through this."

Much to my mother's chagrin, that's all it took to strengthen my resolve to go back the next day. Ballet El Paso was the only ballet company in West Texas. There was no other place to go. To quit would have hurt me more than it would have hurt Ms. Heuser. It would have given her the last word, and I was not about to do that.

But my daughter was not fighting a crotchety old woman who tried to motivate her students by denying them opportunities to dance. She was fighting the snippets of lily-white competition dancers with spaghetti-like limbs, served up by the algorithms of Instagram and TikTok. In their videos they spin, they kick, they jump, their faces frozen in toothy beauty-pageant smiles.

It didn't work to demand that she turn off her phone or to admit that if social media had been around when I was her age, I would have been so depressed by what I'd seen that I would have never become a professional dancer. (Add to that: When I was her age, I was drunk on wine coolers, crawling out of windows and into Joe's bed. And if John Hughes movies were a reliable indicator, I was a late bloomer. Thank God social media wasn't around back then.)

"Those are just tricks," I'd tell her. "That's not what it means to be a dancer."

But what did it mean to be a dancer?

In Italy, I danced with two very different companies. ATERBalletto was the big leagues. Centrally situated in Reggio Emilia, ATER was a private company housed in the beautiful theater in the main piazza. Unlike most of the small private ballet companies in Italy, ATER offered a full season of work. In practical terms, this meant a monthly paycheck and a contract that spanned several months. We had a company masseuse who accompanied us when we went on tour. And not only were we equipped with an ample supply of pointe shoes, but at the start of the winter season, a representative from Freeds of London came to trace our feet and make recommendations for our special orders. Even our makeup was provided for us.

The repertoire was chock-full of top choreographers such as

Jiří Kylián, Balanchine, and Béjart. Rehearsals started on time and ended on time. Most of the dancers were Italian, although a few were French. I was the only American. It was my first professional experience in which most of the dancers were better than I was, and dancing alongside them, trying to keep up, improved my technique drastically. It was here that I executed a rond de jambe so perfect that replaying it in my mind two decades later still gave me a thrill.

With ATER, I danced in some of the most beautiful theaters in Italy. But I only saw them from the stage. Every dark abyss of an audience looked the same. Ditto for the interior of a dressing room and the inside of a bus.

Fabula Saltica, the other company I danced for, was a different kind of experience. Fabula Saltica was part of a communal theater financed by civic funds in its home city of Rovigo. Theater heads commissioned operas and ballets that often favored Italian composers and choreographers.

Fabula Saltica didn't have its own studio space. Sometimes we rehearsed in a rented dance studio outside the city center. One year a makeshift dance floor, constructed in the ballroom of a senior center, served as our rehearsal space. It wasn't closed off from the rest of the center, and curious elderly Italians often gathered to watch and ask questions, hobbling toward us in their walkers, a slow inevitable crowding.

Here, too, I was the only American, and it was only because of the tireless efforts of the director Claudio and his assistant Pia that I was allowed to work in Italy in the first place. In Rovigo, there was no money for shoes or makeup or massage therapists. Dancers were hired for specific performances—six weeks here, three months there. Fabula Saltica consisted of Claudio, Pia, and another core dancer who doubled as associate director and rehearsal assistant. When a ballet required more warm bodies, they turned to call their roster of friends.

Tours were chaotic and poorly organized. There was no bus. Claudio would rent a van, and his assistant would follow in her car. Every time we'd drive to a new city, we'd get lost. (Although Claudio insisted that if we arrived at our location, we didn't get lost, did we? Getting lost would have meant we never got there.)

When we did eventually arrive in a new city, there was an unspoken rule that everyone had an hour or two to explore the main piazza before meeting in the theater. The other dancers knew which delicacies were specific to each region, and it was important to sample what each new province had to offer.

Nothing started "on time." There was no "on time." If we missed the train, we hung around and smoked cigarettes until the next one came. At night after the performance, we would gather at an outdoor osteria or trattoria to sample more local fare. Dinners ran late, often until one o'clock in the morning or later, and the end of the night was usually marked by singing. It was very Italian.

Unlike with ATER, every performance I danced with Fabula Saltica was unique. We performed in the big cities: on Piazza Barberini in Rome, at Castello Sforza in Milan, and on Belvedere, the hill that overlooks Florence. We performed in small cities and in villages so tiny even the Italian dancers hadn't heard of them. In one town there was only hot water in the dressing rooms, in another, only cold. (It's better to have only cold water). In another town, the stage was so small some of our scenery wouldn't fit. We asked the only café in the village if we could borrow the only table they had for the performance. Thrilled, the owner and his sons closed shop early to help us move our new prop up the hill and into the theater.

We danced in the middle of castle ruins on a stage constructed just for us. We danced at an amphitheater with hedges instead of stadium seats. The architect (or gardener?) had populated the hedges with marble busts as a captive audience, and the living ticket holders had to sit in the aisles.

Another time we danced in the amphitheater at the house—now a museum—built for Italian poet Gabriele d'Annunzio. The house sat on twenty-two acres of land, and the amphitheater overlooked Lake Garda. In the final sequence of the ballet, I had to execute a series of jumps upstage. If I applied just the right amount of force, I could jump high enough to have an unobstructed view of the lake and stay suspended in air long enough to enjoy it. I had a fifty-fifty success rate, which perfectly described my time in that country.

Italy created a harmony in my body, a virtuous cycle I felt in my gut—literally. It started with the food. With so many dishes that were new to me, it was impossible to count calories or track foods on the daily diet lists I'd kept since my San Francisco Ballet days. I didn't have access to a scale either. Although even if I did, I wouldn't have been able to read it. The conversion of kilos to pounds felt more like a riddle than simple math.

I'd been weighing myself since sixth grade, and now for the first time since then, there was no outside number by which to judge my body's progress or to measure its failure. I had to depend on how I felt, and to do that, I had to figure out how I was feeling. Was I tired? Was I energized? Was I hungry?

My body recalibrated from the inside out. For the first time, my body looked the way I'd always wanted it to look, but only because I felt the way I'd always wanted to feel—like a shining ball of light, like a pretty girl.

While the meals helped in their small way—fresher ingredients and regular mealtimes made for optimal digestion—the real catalyst that helped me overcome my body issues happened by accident.

Unlike in Germany and Iceland, where classes and rehearsals were conducted in English, life in Italy transpired in Italian. For the first two years, I had no idea what was going on. The language barrier was part of it, but mostly Italian life mystified me. The things I thought were important—traffic laws, for example, or functioning train-station clocks—were considered irrelevant, while other details, such as the authenticity of the lace collars on the corps de ballet dancers' costumes, were valued on a level beyond my comprehension.

I was constantly doing the wrong thing, and my list of petty crimes was extensive. I stirred broken spaghetti with a metal spoon, opened windows that faced the sea, waited for the lights to change before I crossed the street. I couldn't intuit what was expected of me until I unexpectedly did the wrong thing.

The only voice that didn't need translating was that of my inner artist, which had started to sing louder than my inner critic. The more the artist spoke, the easier it was to ignore the critic and the more I ignored the critic, the better I felt in my body. I didn't care anymore if others thought that my neck was short and my ribs were wide. What mattered was that my body was strong, limber, and healthy.

Chiara already knows these stories, but here's the dirty secret I haven't told her: The end result was exhilarating, but the journey was exhausting. Nothing ever matched up with my expectations, intentions, or assumptions. It never happened on a timetable that fit any kind of logic or predictability. And sometimes, the waiting, the process, the attempt, was so excruciating, the road so meandering, the final goal so elusive, that I felt I would trade it all—ancient Roman baths, after-parties with nine-course meals, an osteria in Venice that only opened to those who could find the unmarked door and reproduce the secret knock—I would trade it all for something as safe and stable as a mundane office job. Here the simple math was easy: the contracts weren't long enough and the paychecks weren't big enough to sustain life as an artist. Not even finding my artist's voice and my dancer's body was enough.

I'd never told Chiara this part before because it made me sound ungrateful and made me feel guilty. I knew I wasn't ungrateful. I knew what I had, and I knew how hard I worked to get it. But I didn't know how to keep having it.

Days passed without a text.

"She'll be okay, right?" I asked Matt.

The texts that followed came in nonsequential snippets: an excited message about 7-Eleven offering free slushies on July 11. A screenshot of a possible bank scam. She should just ignore it, right? A description of a horrible teen romance she watched with her roommate. It was nicer than watching a movie she liked by herself, she admitted. Nothing about ballet.

"I think she's okay," Matt said.

Then, after two days of radio silence, confirmation.

Love you mama today was great

In my career as a dancer, I was also noted for my balance, honed after my stint with ATERBalletto. I'd start with a demi plié, feel my connection to gravity before moving to a relevé passé or piqué arabesque. I only progressed to the next step if I felt confident I'd succeed.

By contrast, Chiara, aka "Balance Queen," struck a pose as if she were anchored to the center of the Earth and tethered to the clouds, as if her balance were a foregone conclusion and all she had to do was fulfill her destiny. Sometimes she'd wobble left to right and back again, the way a pendulum comes to stillness. But it always looked as though she could stay there forever. When she finally descended, she did so gracefully, as if it were her choice.

At the end of Chiara's summer intensive, Matt and I flew to Philadelphia to bring her back home. As part of our visit, Matt insisted on showing us his old college stomping grounds in New Jersey.

Princeton was only a forty-five-minute drive north of Philly. It was a small campus compared to the universities Chiara had seen during her summer intensives. The buildings were majestically old and idyllic. It looked like a movie set or a fairy tale. Nearly every building had a backstory.

"This was my eating club, Cottage." Matt pointed to a red-bricked mansion with white-trimmed windows. "We had a pool table and even a tap room downstairs."

"For tap dancing?" Chiara asked, possibly remembering Matt had gotten his start as a tap-dancing sheep.

"Uh, no. For beer." Matt eyed her while she did the math in her head.

"But you were only—"

"Never mind that! It was a different time. Here, let me show you the theater where I did dance."

He launched into reminiscing.

"The summer between junior and senior year, I knew I didn't want to spend it back in Tampa. So I got a job in the chemistry library shelving books for about five bucks an hour. The dorms had been closed for the summer, and my library job didn't pay enough to cover rent for an apartment, but I had a plan. As president of the Princeton Triangle Club, I had keys to the theater, costume shop, and the warehouse used for building scenery.

"The costume shop was the best for sleeping," he told us as we walked across the green, startling black squirrels who scampered across the lawn. "It was full of sixty years' worth of old costumes and dusty old blankets that could be piled up like a mattress. Sometimes I slept in the office. There was a couch in there, and I'd put the cushions on the floor and sleep on those. Once I even slept in the aisle on the floor of the theater."

"They allowed you to sleep in the theater?"

"Oh, no. It wasn't allowed at all, and I was constantly worried that the campus police would sniff me out. That's why I kept changing locations." His eyes twinkled. "I'd read enough spy novels to know you gotta keep moving so they can't get a beat on you."

"Why? Why didn't you just stay with a friend?"

Matt looked back at us as if the answer were obvious. "Because being on campus gave me access to dance studios. At night, everything was deserted. I had the whole place to myself. Even if I didn't have the right keys, I could always find an unlocked door. Once I even climbed through a window. I wanted to improve, and I knew I needed to get better but didn't know how, exactly. I'd repeat the exercises I'd been taught in modern class. You know, you're not sure what the next steps are but you know you have to do something. And then you do it. You make a change and then the steps present themselves."

There were no doors left unlocked anymore. We had to peer through a window at McCarter Theater and use our imagination. It wasn't hard, though. I could see a young Matt, long hair in his face, running and leaping onstage in his white tube socks and old basketball jersey. I could picture him, a young, naively ambitious, and optimistic college student, bucking the trend. The shine inside him matched the ghost light from above. Why go to law school or get an MBA when you could be a *dancer*?

"You make it sound so easy."

Matt shook his head. "Oh, it wasn't easy. And I was terrible. For like, the first two years I danced, I had no idea what I was doing. But you know, you keep at it. You find out what you're good at, and doors open from there. When you've got the itch to dance, you gotta scratch it."

That's what it meant to be a dancer.

MOTHER GINGER

IT WAS HALLOWEEN NIGHT, AND JOHN AND WAYNE HAD TWO
hours to figure out what costume to wear. Last year they dressed
as each other, an inside joke lost on everyone except their closest
friends. This year, the twins hoped to dress up as tethered souls
from the horror movie *Us*, an easy-enough costume as long as we
could find a red hoodie and a pair of red sweats.

In the car on the way to Target, John furiously pecked mes-
sages into his phone.

"Jordan is ghosting me," he said. "When I asked him at school
about trick-or-treating, he made it sound like he was going with
someone else. He wouldn't give me any details. Now he won't
answer any of my texts."

I was shocked. Jordan had been a best friend since first
grade.

"What does Wayne say?"

John shook his head. "He doesn't know anything either. But I
heard Jordan and Eli talking to Marcus. I know they have plans."
He looked down at his phone again.

I offered explanations. Maybe Jordan's phone was dead.
Maybe Eli had to check with his parents. Marcus would never
leave him out. John countered with more arguments.

"You don't understand. When you've hit puberty, you don't want to be friends with a twelve-year-old who looks like he's still in fourth grade."

For my twins, puberty couldn't come soon enough. Unfortunately, from the looks of things, it would be a while.

"They're going to invite Wayne and not me. They don't want me to come. But they don't know how to tell me. I know it's not easy to be friends with twins. Especially when you want to just invite one of them." He sighed. "Plus, I've been kind of annoying lately."

He listed all the ways he had been a pest: making jokes when they'd asked him to stop; sending multiple texts when friends didn't answer right away. The list was extensive.

"Sometimes I'll go into a game on Roblox, and they leave when I get there."

There was a lot to consider. I couldn't imagine his buddies would try to get rid of him, but John had obviously noticed the social cues, even if he hadn't respected them. What if he was right? Sometimes friends moved on and you had to get new ones. What if this was one of those times?

"You know, when I was about your age, I had a group of friends. We called ourselves 'The Fantastic Four.' We did everything together. Then one day, I opened my math book and there was a note. *YOU ARE OUT OF THE FANTASTIC FOUR.* And that was it. My friends wouldn't talk to me anymore. Actually, there was just one friend—Holly—who wouldn't talk to me, and she told the others not to be my friend. So if she was around, the other girls ignored me."

John was stunned. "Really? Why?"

I sighed. It was still a painful memory. "Well, Holly said I was always showing off. I'd practice choreography on the playground during recess. But I wasn't showing off. I had such a hard time remembering steps. I needed all the rehearsal I could get. After that, I ate lunch in the library for the rest of the school year because I didn't want to sit in the cafeteria by myself." My voice brightened. "But I found new friends. Like Sofia at ballet. And my friend Andrea. You know her, the one with the Australian Shepherds."

There was a lot more to the story. But it wasn't exactly age-appropriate, even if John and I were the same age when it happened.

The truth was that Holly, Colleen, Lisa, and I were friends in name only. As a group we did little more than discuss the TV shows we weren't allowed to watch. The real glue of our friendship seemed to be that we spent most of our time in the same place: Mrs. Vogel's sixth-grade classroom.

One day Colleen came to school with a book she'd found under her parents' bed. Judging by the cover, you would not find this book in the library at Eastwood Heights Elementary. Under a title in flowery cursive was an ample-breasted woman in a plaid halter top and jean shorts even shorter than the ones Chrissy wore in *Three's Company*—one of the shows my friends and I weren't allowed to see.

Colleen glanced at the door to our classroom, where Mrs. Vogel stood guard. "It's all about sex," she said.

"Lemme see." I grabbed the book and flipped to a dog-eared passage.

There on the page a guy named Derek was stroking his you-know-what in front of an enthusiastic redhead named Candy. By the second paragraph, which was filled with words I'd previously only seen etched on bathroom stalls, Derek and Candy were *doing it*. Just reading made me feel tingly in a way I hadn't known could happen.

"Can I borrow this?" I asked, already shoving the book into my lunch box.

At home, under the covers with a carefully balanced flashlight on my pillow, I read about this Derek guy. He was a well-endowed gigolo who was a bit of a workaholic. I imagined he looked like one of the Village People—the construction worker, maybe. Derek was on a quest for true love. He agonized that women only liked him for his foot-long manhood, and he kept searching for Mrs. Right—at the laundromat, the grocery store, the beach, the bus stop. Derek satisfied women everywhere he went. But none of it was true love. So, he kept looking.

I was appalled and fascinated. The bodies I knew—the ones that could do triple pirouettes and piqué arabesques—weren't sexualized. They were instruments of movement, sensual in a different way. In ballet, an arched back wasn't a reaction; it was intentional. Legs lifted and spiraled as part of leaps and turns. They were never just "akimbo," which, as far as I could tell, meant "just lying there."

I wrapped the book in lime-green shelf paper and wrote *TINA AND TONY GO TO THE ZOO* across the top in block letters. It seemed the safest way to circulate the book around Mrs. Vogel's class.

It was October. I was still taking ballet classes with Renée, who had explained to Dee Bee and me that the four teenagers who'd been cast last year as buffoons in Ballet El Paso's "Mother Ginger" variation had grown too big over the summer. She'd widened her hands as she described the kind of growth spurts they'd had—inches in widths and curves, not just in height. I had never been in *The Nutcracker* before, and if I could do cartwheels and walkovers, I had a good chance at the part.

Cartwheels were easy. You just had to keep your legs straight. But a walkover required flexibility, strength, and coordination. When Dee Bee did them, she looked like a slinky going down the stairs. When I did them, I looked as if I was purposely trying to fall on my head.

On the day of the audition, Ms. Heuser stood at the front of the studio, frowning as always. Her crimson-red hair sat on top of her head in a tangle.

"Blanca! You look like a baby elephant when you jump. You've lost all talent. Maybe tennis could help you lose weight," she said to a dancer with a tiny waist but big hips.

The dancer stood very still in fifth position and stared straight ahead. Her cheeks turned red. She looked like the type who refused to cry.

I'd never been to an audition before, but I had been to Ms. Heuser's classes. I knew it was never okay to show disappointment, fear, or even relief unless it was part of the choreography.

Ms. Heuser waved her hand, dismissing the dancer. "Next group!" she said to David.

It wasn't like the placement audition that Sofia and I would take a few years later at San Francisco Ballet School. Nor was it like the cattle call auditions Dee Bee and I would attend as professional dancers. This audition was simple: the four dancers with the best walkovers would be cast as Mother Ginger's buffoons.

In some versions of "Mother Ginger," the dancers are very young children. They skip and wave and look adorable. Ms. Heuser would have none of that. If she put dancers onstage, they were going to dance. Cute wasn't enough.

One girl didn't get to audition at all. As soon as we stood up, Ms. Heuser exclaimed, "She looks like a weed! What am I going to do with a cornstalk?" She made a sweeping motion with her hand.

David translated. "Too tall. Maybe a mouse this year." The girl started to walk to the back of the studio, but Mr. David stopped her. "Come back tomorrow for the battle scene auditions." The girl bit her lip and picked up her dance bag.

Now we were five dancers for four spots.

The other girls didn't need to suck in their flat stomachs, but they did anyway, holding their chins up, just the way Ms. Heuser instructed. ("Like you're wearing a diamond necklace at a fancy party.") We were all the same age, but they looked like four miniature ballerinas, while I looked like a little kid. All knees and elbows.

"Show me walkovers," Ms. Heuser said.

The first three girls flipped from one side of the studio to the other, Dee Bee among them. They easily passed the test, even though one girl did all her walkovers to the left. Ms. Heuser didn't like that, but I guess she assumed that if Raquel could do beautiful walkovers to the left, it was only a matter of time before she could do them to the right. But Sofia, long and willowy, lacked the strength to push out of her backbends. She didn't get to cross to the other side of the studio. Unfortunately, I wasn't much better. Without the coordination to look graceful, my walkovers thudded on the sprung floor.

"I can't put you onstage like that. You must be able to do walkovers." Ms. Heuser shook her head. I couldn't tell if she was talking to Sofia or me.

David translated again. "It's up to you guys. Whoever can do walkovers by Thanksgiving will get to dance."

Our first "Mother Ginger" rehearsal was scheduled on Halloween night. Company dancers still sweaty from class filled the narrow brown hall. Sofia shuffled a deck of cards for another round of Crazy Eights with her friends. I scratched out some math problems in a spiral notebook.

David bounded down the hall with a tape recorder in his hand. He wore a bumblebee costume with springy antennae affixed to his head with a headband. He even had a stinger. Something about his brusque manner let us know that the costume was part of a joke that was not for us. Perhaps he had some mysterious grown-up party to go to after rehearsal.

"Mother Ginger!" he announced. His antennae bounced up and down. "Follow me."

Sofia put her deck of cards away. I packed up my homework, pulling my leotard down as I stood up, hoping to hide my underwear. We marched behind David like little ducklings.

Ms. Heuser's choreography for "Mother Ginger" was a story. One by one, we emerged from Mother Ginger's skirt in a series of chaînés, posing with our arms outstretched while César, who was so beautiful he'd been Miss Gay El Paso three years in a row, wobbled above us on stilts and beamed as our proud mother.

For the next several phrases of music, we stage-fought over center stage. When the tone of the music changed, so did our stage mood. Peace was made between the buffoons. With partnered lifts and cancan-like emboîtés, we grinned and romped in formation, circling Mother Ginger with the most challenging steps we could manage at eleven years old.

Usually, ballet felt like a game whose rules I understood but couldn't follow—like the difference between a dictionary definition and using the word in a complete sentence. In the ballet studio, I was constantly doing the wrong thing. My elbows sagged when they should have been lifted. When the rest of the class would chassé to the right, I'd end up galloping to the left. But the steps we danced for "Mother Ginger" were different.

Nobody needed to tell me that I'd look even more mischievous if I raised my shoulders and tilted my head. Or that I could feign staged innocence if I batted my eyelashes. Dee Bee was my partner for much of the dance. She was as much of an actress as I was. The more we rehearsed, the more creative we became. We could be angels or we could be naughty. Suddenly, it was fun to dance. Nobody came out and said that I was doing well, but that's something else I figured out. Silence was praise.

Ms. Heuser played favorites. It was evident in how she looked at some girls and ignored others. She favored her company dancers over her students, and she favored her own students over dancers from other studios. My only chance to be cast in "Mother Ginger" would be if I mastered walkovers before Sofia did.

Our front lawn was perfect for practicing. The grass was more forgiving than the blacktop at school or the Marley floor at ballet. And no one was watching or judging—unless you counted my mother. I knew she was trying to help, but it was annoying. None of her comments made sense.

"You need to reach out with your leg," she repeated for the tenth time. She never used the right ballet terms. She said things like "stand with your foot out" instead of tendu and "kick your leg high" instead of grand battement.

I took a deep breath and stretched toward the sky. Tumbling forward, my legs landed with a double thud. I pushed to stand. Technically, it was a walkover, but I was too slow getting up.

I tried again. *Thud. Thud.* Stuck.

"Don't let the right leg come down. Make it reach up into the next walkover."

It sounded ridiculous. That would be like a one-footed back-bend. Surely, I would fall if I tried that.

"One more time," my mother said. "You can do it."

I stood at the edge of the lawn. From tendu front, I stepped forward and let my legs fly behind me and over my head. My left leg landed. My right leg reached out into the next tendu, and then I stood up. It happened so quickly. As if it required no strength at all. Just faith.

My mother clapped her hands. "You got it! That's it! That's how the other girls do it!"

I scampered to the edge of the lawn to practice again. It wasn't like a slinky clunking down the stairs at all. It was like a pinwheel blowing in the wind with one rotation propelling into the next. With a broad smile and a tendu to the front, I propelled myself across the grass.

Sometimes ballet's learning curve is like a jagged line, like finally getting the hang of a double pirouette. After your first perfect double, it might be a while before you land the next one. Other times it's like a light switch, with speed and strength working in tandem.

Once your brain figures out how to do a perfect walkover, you never do a bad one ever again.

The switch had been flipped. I could do walkovers both backward and forward. I could do a fast walkover and a slow, controlled walkover. I could even do them to the left.

At some point between Thanksgiving and our first *Nutcracker*, I reached under my desk to pull out my math book. As I opened it to the assigned page, an index card fell out onto the floor. In capital letters, it read, *YOU ARE OUT OF THE FANTASTIC FOUR.*

My face stung, and I knew I was turning red. I looked over to

Holly. She jerked her head away, pretending she hadn't been watching me.

At lunchtime on the blacktop, the other girls ignored me.

"Hey, guys. Stop playing!"

"Do you hear anything?" Holly asked Colleen, who shook her head. They linked arms and walked away. It was not unlike Ms. Heuser calling to César to show Mrs. Armendáriz who was in control.

After school I caught Lisa's attention. "What happened? What did I do?"

Lisa shrugged. "Well, you're always dancing. It's like you think you're better than everyone else. Like you're always showing off."

My jaw dropped. I wasn't showing off. I was trying to keep up.

The next day during the bustle before school, Holly said in a voice louder than necessary, "Look! I made a new cover for *The Book*!" She held it up for all to see. She'd replaced my lime-green cover with shocking pink but kept the title *TINA AND TONY GO TO THE ZOO*. The handwriting was suspiciously similar to the letters on the index card I'd found inside my math book.

Our class clown grabbed it out of her hand. He was in mid-sneer when Mrs. Vogel came up behind him and deftly snatched the book away. She didn't ask any questions. She just put it on top of her desk and opened her roll book as if nothing had happened. I was grateful the title wasn't in my handwriting anymore.

Every day after lunch, Mrs. Vogel would sit on the corner of her desk and read books to us like *Charlotte's Web* and *Watership Down*. But that afternoon she stood, holding *The Book* in its original form, revealing curvy flesh on the cover.

We sat as still as possible, unsure what tirade would follow. Would she call our parents? Could we get expelled?

"This book!" Mrs. Vogel shook it at us and then shook her

head, dabbing at her eyes. She was crying. "Oh, children! Making love is something very special and very wonderful. It's not like what's in this book."

Holy frijoles. Mrs. Vogel has had sex.

Momentarily forgetting I was friendless, I tried to catch Colleen's eye. *Mrs. Vogel has been naked with Mr. Vogel! But not like Derek was naked with his landlady.*

Colleen was scrunched down at her desk. Her face was bright pink, much like the pink on the cover Holly had made. If Mrs. Vogel hadn't known before whose book it was, she certainly knew it now.

"Making love is a treasured experience between a husband and wife." She choked between sobs. "Children, this book is trash. And it is my job to make sure that you know that the real world is not like this."

Oh! That was truly disappointing to hear. I knew stuff like this didn't happen in real life, at least not in El Paso but maybe in a more exciting city, like Albuquerque. I knew it was fantasy in the same way I knew that spiders couldn't spin webs with words in them. But just as I believed that Charlotte and Wilbur exemplified true friendship, I wanted to believe that sex was exactly the way Derek experienced it: exciting, fun, and leaving everyone breathless afterward.

That afternoon in the dressing room, I watched the company dancers change. Like superheroes, they shed the costumes of their ordinary daytime identities as waitresses and substitute teachers. They donned colorful Lycra leotards gathered in the front with safety pins and wore ripped black tights with runs that looked like battle scars. Their curves were calf muscles and quadriceps, not hips and bosoms. These were the people I wanted to be like, not Derek and Candy or Holly and Colleen.

Inside the studio, David practiced double tours from his Russian variation. Sometimes he landed in a perfect fifth position. Sometimes he wobbled. But regardless of the outcome, he took a deep breath and tried again. Renée rehearsed the piqué turns from the coda of her Sugar Plum Fairy solo. Everyone was trying to be the best they could be.

In some ways the older dancers were just as uninhibited as Derek and all the other naked people in Colleen's book. They stood in the nude in the dressing room as they discussed a difficult step or a juicy nugget of gossip. And I'd seen firsthand last year during *Sleeping Beauty* when one of the soloists had a quick change. She took off her whole costume in a corner near the prop table. Even though she was in plain sight of everybody backstage—even the stagehands—nobody stared or said a word. She peeled off one tutu and donned the next as nonchalantly as my mother changed her earrings.

If this had been Derek's world, that ballerina would have succumbed to her animal instincts with a stagehand up against the prop table. She would have been late for her entrance, and her bodice would have been missing some hooks. But of course, no one I knew in real life seemed to struggle with the same impulse-control issues that Derek and his lady friends contended with. It was ridiculous to imagine. A pig talking to his spider friend was more believable.

Normally, I came to ballet already in my class uniform, but that afternoon I wanted to know what it would feel like to change in the dressing room, in front of everybody else. I crouched in the corner, pulling off my underwear when I pulled off my jeans. I stretched my pink tights over my bare skin. It felt different, as if I were still naked. I didn't feel brave. I just felt exposed. When it came time to put on my leotard, I faced the wall, even though I knew the rest of the girls were too busy chattering to notice.

Maybe the middle way wasn't about what a body could say but what a body could do. Evidently both Derek and the Vogels did the same stuff with their bodies—at least in a general sense. But Mrs. Vogel seemed to think that a naked body could only talk to one's spouse—everything else was shameful—while Derek's body yammered on to (and with) anybody who would listen.

Sitting on the bench in the dressing room, I watched the older girls. Their bodies radiated. But unlike the women in Colleen's book, they did not beckon. Each dancer was a sun basking in her own glow. I tugged on my leotard, forgetting that there was no underwear to hide.

In my story to John, I left out the part about Colleen's book. I left in the part about the walkovers.

"Holly never talked to me again. Not even at our twentieth high school reunion."

His mouth dropped open. "Really?"

I'd seen Holly from across the room. Her eyes passed over me as if I weren't there. I wondered if she remembered that I'd been "The One Who Went to San Francisco." Or maybe she hadn't kept tabs on me after I left. Maybe our friendship had been one-sided, something that had meant more to me than it had to her. I did see Lisa at that reunion. We'd become friends again in ninth grade and Facebook friends as adults, but I never asked her if she remembered what had happened in Mrs. Vogel's class.

"So you never got your revenge?" John asked.

"No," I said a little too sadly. But that wasn't exactly true either. Mrs. Vogel had known I'd been ostracized by our friend group, and I think she suspected Colleen's book had been the reason. After *The Book* had been discovered, she was uncharacteristically lenient with me while increasing her impatience with the rest of our class—special treatment I readily took advantage of. Ms. Heuser's late rehearsals meant that I was always behind on homework.

To cover up my lateness, I submitted history homework with math exercises or attached math problems to my spelling quizzes, hoping Mrs. Vogel would just think of me as disorganized. It worked to the extent that my grade never suffered the way it would have if another student had turned in late work. At the time I thought Mrs. Vogel had felt sorry for me. But looking back, a more plausible explanation was she thought of me as the moral compass who stood up to the sexual deviants of sixth grade. I didn't question the favoritism, but I knew Holly was responsible for it.

To John, I gave a different side of the truth. "Those girls weren't my real friends. I practiced walkovers because doing well in ballet was important to me. And my work paid off. Know what else? Sofia never held it against me that I got the part instead of her. That's a real friend."

At Target, we bought a hoodie and sweatpants. Now all John needed to complete his costume was a pair of scissors, unless he was going to stay home and watch TV, in which case his outfit was complete. Jordan still hadn't responded to the barrage of texts and neither had any of his friends. Fighting back tears, John scrolled through his phone.

I wished I could be the kind of parent who reassured her kids by telling them everything was going to be okay. But I had never been able to do that.

When the twins were born, they were so tiny. Matt and I spent hours standing over their Isolettes. The hours became days. The days became months. We watched as they were hooked up to the machines and monitors that kept them alive. Sometimes their hearts beat often enough and sometimes they didn't. Sometimes they breathed deeply enough; too often they didn't. I knew I could not make any promises about their future. I still wouldn't make promises.

But I did know about resilience. I knew about loyalty. I knew how to listen to your heart and take deep breaths when things got tough.

"Look, if we get home and it turns out that Jordan and Wayne and all the guys have already made arrangements, we'll make a great night of it, just you and me. We'll watch *The Shining*, and I'll let you eat all the candy you want."

John squeezed my arm. "Mom." He looked at me and gave my hand a little pat. "No offense. But that is so lame."

At home a bemused Wayne confirmed radio silence from the group text. It might be a night for *The Shining* after all.

Suddenly, there was a ruckus at the door. Pounding. Yelling. It didn't sound like trick-or-treaters. It sounded like a riot. I opened the door to an Elvis, a Dementor, a ninja, and a thing in a pink-feathered hat and rhinestone sunglasses (Elton John, perhaps?)—all taller than I was. They yelled over each other. Their fragments formed a story.

"John! Wayne!"

"I got locked out of my phone—"

"Come on!"

"—faster to just run here!"

"We didn't want you to think we left—"

"Let's go!"

The gang was all here and ready to go.

John's gaze locked onto mine, and his eyes glistened with relief.

"Mom! I'm not ready!" He grabbed his hoodie out of the bag and pulled at the tags. Now it was my turn to give him a squeeze.

"It's okay, honey. Don't worry. They'll wait for you. They're your friends."

WALTZ OF THE FLOWERS

WHEN I WAS FOURTEEN YEARS OLD, MS. HEUSER SENT ME A bouquet of flowers. No one had ever sent me flowers before, unless you counted the carnations from Skaggs grocery store, stained blue and wrapped in cellophane. Those were from my mother. Of course, those didn't count.

Bright-orange lilies with pointy petals and fat pink roses were flanked by big, happy sunflowers and balanced with sprigs of baby's breath. Not one flower was out of place. Each bloom was distinct and deliberately positioned, like a synchronized dance. I stared at the assortment of stems and blooms. They looked like a corps de ballet shimmering on center stage, praising me and performing for me at the same time.

The card was penned in the crooked cursive of Ms. Heuser. I had always associated her angular handwriting with abrasiveness and volatility.

Thank you, the card began.

As long as I had danced for her, I had watched her play favorites. Being in her good graces didn't manifest in effusive praise or prized roles. It usually just meant fewer insults.

My mother would point out all the nearly imperceptible ways Ms. Heuser would pit one dancer against another . . . how she would berate her students until they stopped listening.

"The thing is, she's often right. I sit there in the rehearsal and she will say, 'Oh, Madeleine!'" Even my mother could do a spot-on impersonation of Ms. Heuser. "'You need to do it like *dees*.' And I'd think to myself, *She's right*. I hate to agree with her. But she was right. That's exactly what Madeleine needed to do." My mother, who knew nothing of épaulment but had the discerning eye of a balletomane, could see the difference. "Of course, by that time, the dancers were so tired of her. They were so angry and hurt they wouldn't listen. I don't blame them."

The year before I started high school, Ms. Heuser fired all her dancers. Sofia and I were headed to study at San Francisco Ballet for the summer. We followed the drama in the papers from articles my mother clipped and mailed to me in the dorms. It was front-page news. Disgruntled dancers, angry over long hours and mistreatment, raised their concerns with the board and told their stories to the press. Ms. Heuser retaliated by firing them.

Having turned her back on the dancers she'd raised—some from kindergarten through adulthood—Ms. Heuser showered her attention on the new crop. She promoted Sofia, Dee Bee, me, and the rest of our class to junior apprentices for a company that had no other dancers.

For *The Nutcracker*, Ms. Heuser fleshed out her new company with soloists from Mexico, journeymen from other regional ballet companies, and her advanced students. I was still Fritz. Sofia was still the favorite cousin to Dee Bee's Clara. But now we were eligible for new roles: "Waltz of the Flowers."

The choreography was simple. Twelve dancers waltzed in unison: forward, back, then side to side. Repeat. Something to the right was often followed by something to the left. On the fast music, we did fast steps. On the slow music, we did slow ones. Back when Dee Bee and I had private classes with Renée, she'd taught us the opening sequence as part of our center exercises. It had been revelatory. Those swooshes and dips had names and directions and counts. Each one led into the next, the way letters formed words and words formed sentences. I'd seen this choreography performed by so many dancers onstage, and now my own limbs were speaking the same language, telling the same story. I don't remember learning how to read, but it must have felt like this.

By the time I was cast to dance as a waltz flower, I knew the steps as well as I knew the Pledge of Allegiance. That's how I knew even though Sofia was in the back row, she'd been cast as one of the flowers who did the most dancing. It's also how I knew my place—middle flower, second row—was where they put the weak dancers, the wilted bloom in the middle of the bunch. The spot even had its own name: the Dunce Flower.

I was disappointed, but at least I wasn't the understudy, the dancer who would only dance if someone got injured. That undesirable distinction went to Sandy.

Sandy was quiet and dependable, one of several dancers who hung around Ballet El Paso. They were too old to be students and too familiar to be offered company contracts, as if Ms. Heuser wanted to punish them for their loyalty. There was never a shortage of eager pleasers in this echelon of dancers who were neither on their way up nor on their way out, and Ms. Heuser often cast them in roles that required a dancer's grace but not a dancer's technique.

They were the first to be insulted when she was angry and the first she'd turn to when she needed something. Decades later, they were the ones who visited when she was homebound, the ones who organized a meal train after her stroke or spent time with her when she was moved to hospice.

Maybe it was because my mother pointed out the ways Ms. Heuser used and abused her dancers, or maybe I just instinctively knew that reverence and respect were the surest way to earn her scorn. Either way, I knew it would backfire if I showed I was too eager to please.

David clapped his hands to start the rehearsal. I thought he'd teach us the steps that I'd already learned, but he began at the very beginning: the harp solo where the dancers run out and spiral around, meeting in the middle to be petals of a giant bloom that blossomed open, then closed before the twelve of us took our places. No one wanted to be the center flower—she had to kneel downstage, open into a deep backbend, and hold it for several counts. I was one of the dancers who had to balance en pointe in fourth position. I knew from four years of being en pointe that it was very hard to be still in fourth position. I tried to cover up my wobbles by looking up instead of down at the floor.

Ms. Heuser grumbled to David and the rehearsal stopped. The center flower came out of her backbend. I came down off pointe.

"Sandy!"

Sandy jumped to attention.

"Take the middle spot."

Sandy understood before I did. She walked to the center of the studio and stood so close to me I involuntarily moved out of her way. The other dancers folded around her, moving as a coherent whole. She stepped up to fourth position en pointe, and just like that, Sandy was the Dunce Flower, and I was the understudy.

The rehearsal progressed, and David taught the rest of the flowers the steps I already knew. Ms. Heuser watched from her stool at the front of the studio with her arms folded across her chest, looking alternately displeased and disinterested. From time to time, she patted her hair, which today was a tumbleweed of rusty orange. On the sidelines, I wanted to show that I already knew the steps, but there wasn't enough room to dance without bumping into the other flowers.

After the rehearsal, the dancers dispersed. I cautiously approached her stool. I wasn't sure how to tell her she was wrong. I should be dancing, not Sandy.

Shaking her head as if I'd committed some infraction, she spoke in a voice tinged with exasperation.

"You look like a giraffe that is learning to gallop. Why can't you just dance like a pretty girl?"

"Will you put me back in if I come to every rehearsal and learn all the steps?" I asked, hoping this could be like the year I mastered walkovers for "Mother Ginger."

She shrugged. "It's not enough to know the steps. But if you come to every rehearsal and prove yourself, then you can dance one performance."

I thanked her.

I liked a challenge. In seventh grade, I had been placed in a math class in which we were allowed to progress at our own pace. Within two months, I had aced every test in the seventh- and eighth-grade math books. For the next year and a half, I tackled algebra along with thirty other students. Surrounded by all honors kids, I fell squarely in the middle of the pack.

By May of eighth grade, we were ready to jump into tenth-grade-level math. But the school district disagreed and issued an ultimatum. Only those who passed the final exam with a grade of 85 or higher would advance to geometry. The rest would have to take algebra again.

A proctor from the school district's central office came to administer an exam they had designed themselves. For a full hour, the proctor paced back and forth between the desks, peered over shoulders to ensure we didn't cheat, and clacked her heels on the tile, breaking our concentration.

I surprised everyone when the scores came back, and I was one of only six students who'd passed.

I wasn't surprised. No one expected me to get into San Francisco Ballet School either. And I did—with a scholarship. Something magical inside me, the thing that made me special and wonderful, had risen through my ribs, like my own angel wings elevating me. This was how I knew I was exceptional. I didn't have to be the best. Sometimes it was enough to work hard and get lucky. It was like a secret I knew about myself.

Rehearsals progressed as usual. Ms. Heuser called one dancer "deformed" and told another her legs were better suited for water aerobics. It was never clear which barbs were designed to insult and which ones were intended to motivate. Meanwhile, I marked through "Waltz of the Flowers" from the sidelines, ready to step in and displace Sandy at any moment. Ms. Heuser ignored both of us, which could have meant that I'd already proved myself, or it could have meant that I needed to try harder.

I had never given Ms. Heuser a Christmas present before, but it seemed like a good way to remind her that I was flower-ready without actually broaching the subject. Perhaps a ballet-themed coffee mug with hippo ballerinas would do the trick. I hoped she wouldn't think the cartoon drawings were too fat to be in tutus.

Before I knew it, it was opening night. Ms. Heuser pinned my wig and called me "the best Fritz we've ever had."

Maybe as Clara, Dee Bee got the nutcracker and star billing, but as Fritz I owned the party scene. When the choreography called for it (and even sometimes when it didn't), I pulled her ribbons. When I knew the audience was watching me, I stuck my tongue out at Sandy in her Maid #3 costume behind her back. When I was supposed to give her my trumpet, I refused. The audience laughed.

Just before the "Grandfather Dance," I made sure the soloist who danced the role of the mother, Frau Stahlbaum, could see me when I pulled the strings of Sandy's apron. She gave me a stern stage reprimand, and I bowed a stage apology. When she turned her back, I copied Sandy's waddle, earning another laugh from the audience.

I didn't know if people were born with this ability or they learned it. But I knew I had it. My heart shone through my costume like a spotlight. I could command attention just by willing it. The hairs on the back of my neck were antennae that transmitted orders: *You will watch me.*

During intermission, I took out my pin curls and put my hair in a bun, just in case Sandy fell down the stairs and turned an ankle. She did not. One day in the future, it would be Sandy who would give me a retail job at her dance supply store. It would supplement my meager Ballet El Paso salary and make the difference between making ends meet and buying plane tickets to audition overseas. But right now she was just in my way. I watched her dance the Dunce Flower from the wings.

Before the warm-up of the final performance, I waited for Ms. Heuser outside her office to give her the coffee mug. It was supposed to be a conversation starter. She was supposed to remember her promise. Instead she smiled her thanks and locked the wrapped present in her office. During warm-up, she didn't insult me and didn't actively ignore me. This was a good sign.

When we were dismissed to the dressing rooms, she turned off the lights in the studio and locked the door behind her. I panicked. Someone needed to tell Sandy that she would not be dancing today. I followed Ms. Heuser backstage.

"You promised I could dance in 'Waltz of the Flowers,'" I said, with a confidence I did not have to fake.

She looked at me, surprised, as if trying to make sense of what she'd just heard.

I'd never seen that look before, and in the moment it took her to recover, I understood. She was never going to let me dance. She had not been waiting for me to prove myself. Not only had she given me a fake challenge, but she had forgotten she had done so.

Ms. Heuser looked up at the clock, probably calculating how much time was left to pin wigs and adjust costumes. She paused, and I had the distinct feeling that she was waiting for me to back down. I did not.

"Show me. If you can dance it perfectly, I will let you perform." She raised a finger and looked me straight in the eye. "Perfectly."

I walked to the stage.

"Not here. Come to the studio." She jingled her key ring. I

followed four paces behind, ready to show her what I knew.

In the studio she perched herself on her stool and folded her arms. I walked to the corner, ready to dance. When she pressed the play button on the tape recorder, the woodwinds began to sing.

As many times as I had practiced on the side, I had never thought to practice the entrance. I was surprised at how unsure I was. I knew that the Dunce Flower wasn't the first flower to enter. Nor was she the last, but without other dancers as a reference, I had to guess where to stand and how fast to run. I didn't have the experience to cover my mistakes. I estimated where my spot would be in the opening formation, and when I realized that I was wrong, it showed on my face.

But once the harp finished its arpeggios, I was on terra firma. I knew my steps: front, back, side to side. Repeat. I felt Ms. Heuser's hard gaze, and I answered with pointed feet and strong legs and the same lift in my chin as when I commanded the stage in the party scene as Best Fritz Ever. I was born to do this.

The final phrases of the music involved running back to the opening flower formation, and this time I knew where to stand. This time I did not wobble in fourth position, even though my heart was thumping. I was still breathing hard when she snapped off the tape recorder.

"It wasn't perfect," she said as she lumbered off the stool and started to walk away.

I protested. "I just got confused at the beginning, but it will be different onstage! Please, just give me another chance. I can do it!"

She shook her head. "You'll dance it next year. You'll be ready then."

I held my tears as long as I could.

When she came to pin my wig for Fritz, my eyes were red. I refused to meet her gaze in the mirror.

"I learned how to tie a bow when I was a shop girl at JCPenney's," she said with a bright smile as she took my silk tie and fashioned it into a perfect bow, as if I hadn't already heard all her stories. I didn't say anything.

Onstage I poked Dee Bee on cue. I grabbed her nutcracker and tore off the head, just like the choreography told me to. I tried to pretend that everything was normal . . . like I was still king of the party scene, and this was Christmas Eve. But I didn't look for opportunities to make the audience laugh. I didn't pull at Sandy's apron. My heart wasn't in it.

I didn't put my hair in a bun at intermission or watch from the wings during the second act. I removed my makeup and shrank inside of myself. I sat in a corner near the downstairs dressing rooms while Sofia, Sandy, and the other flowers waltzed onstage. The timbre of the music vibrated from the orchestra pit through the walls. I couldn't hear the applause, but I knew it was there . . . claps and cheers for everybody but me.

My mother was furious.

"Would it kill her to give someone a chance to dance who deserved it?" In her mind, by working so hard and attending every rehearsal, I had deserved a place in "Waltz of the Flowers."

But "deserve" and "earn" are different.

From the doorway of my bedroom, she looked at the flowers Ms. Heuser had given me. "That woman was never going to let you dance that role. She just wanted it to look like your fault instead of her decision." She shook her head. "I'm sorry, honey."

I looked at the card in my hand.

Your adorable gift gives me laughter every morning when I drink my coffee out of your cup, it read. *I love it especially now that I don't have to worry anymore about Sugar Plum Fairies and possible disasters.*

The card continued: *I was immensely sorry to have seen you hurting again about the waltz. When I saw that you were not 100% sure I could not let you dance.*

Ms. Heuser explained that when a corps de ballet danced together, they had to dance as one. They were only as strong as the weakest dancer. Even the smallest mistake pulled the audience's eye. The director's job, she insisted, was to give the audience the best performance she could.

Please don't be discouraged, you'll see that good parts will come your way and your hard work will bring you joy.

This wasn't a thank-you card. It was an apology.

Ms. Heuser was apologizing, and at the same time, she wasn't. My fourteen-year-old brain knew that much. She was telling me I was the weakest dancer, a truth that stung more than all the insults put together. I would have rather been called a duck waiting to lay an egg or told to busk around subway stations dancing for loose change. I could handle her abuse but not her honesty.

I pictured myself dancing the Dunce Flower instead of Sandy. My chin lifted, heart shining. The hairs on the back of my neck tingling like antennae, completely oblivious to my faults.

I saw myself from the audience's point of view—a gangly teenager, more giraffe than ballerina, who flopped around, one beat ahead of everyone else, pulling the audience's collective eye. *Why can't she dance like a pretty girl?* they would have winced with a collective cringe. *Who put her out there?* they would have thought with their collective brain.

My cheeks burned with the humiliation Ms. Heuser claimed

to have spared me. I could see her sitting in her garden in her white linen pantsuit and pink lacquered nails, sipping tea that Gigi poured out for her. With her witch sense, she would know I felt sorry for myself, and it would make her grin to think she'd won.

I knew some of the poses I made didn't look the way they did on other dancers. Too often I flopped to the left when everyone else floated to the right. But when I danced, I always felt beautiful. I glowed from the inside out, and I knew that not everybody could do that, even if they danced the right steps and I didn't.

I wanted ballet to be unquantifiable: *If you can dream it, you can be it!* But really it was just like my algebra test. If you didn't measure up, you didn't pass. The shine I felt on the inside didn't match the shapes I made on the outside. That's why I didn't earn my spot.

If one flower in this giant bouquet was wilted, it's all I would notice. I wouldn't see the six perfect lilies or the eleven other pristine roses. Ms. Heuser was right.

I didn't want to be the giraffe in a bouquet of flowers. I wanted the thing inside me that made me special to rise up and overshadow my lack of technique or poor timing. But it didn't.

Those flowers weren't a gift; they were a reminder. I was not pretty enough to be Clara or good enough to dance instead of Sandy. While Sofia and the rest of my friends shone as flowers, I "pulled the eye." Which was fine, as long as I was playing the comical role of Fritz—but not for anything else.

I hid the card in the back of my bedroom closet under a stack of sweaters. On my desk, the roses looked out. The happy sunflowers shone on. Between sprigs of baby's breath, a tiny green bud waited for its turn to blossom.

GRAND PAS DE DEUX

LIFE WAS GOOD. THE SMALL GRIEVANCES OUTNUMBERED THE big worries. Matt liked his work at the law firm. He was well-suited to be a lawyer, and I was well-suited to work at home. It gave my schedule flexibility to teach ballet and pursue small creative projects while still being available to take kids where they needed to go and listen when they needed someone to talk to. Matt and I still worked favorite movie lines into casual conversation, and we still made lists of the best indie music to choreograph to.

And yet—

At night I still ran through my stage triumphs as I drifted off to sleep. I'd summon the sauté arabesque in the amphitheater that overlooked Lake Garda, the extra-long balance dancing *Coppelía* at an Icelandic senior living facility. I'd replay the helicopter lift when Matt and I had rehearsed the grand pas de deux of the Sugar Plum Fairy. Not as I had experienced it—a jump, a whir, and a dramatic catch—but the way it had looked in the mirror: in slow-motion, my leg like a propeller, an exclamation point at the end of a career. I wanted to remember the thrill of being thrown in the air, the moment of suspension before falling, the expanse of possibility before landing in Matt's arms.

Stepping onto the stage wasn't just an extroverted act. It was a search for something divine, and maybe today was the day I'd find it. If I was done dancing, then I was done searching. That was a terrifying thought. Might as well be death.

Then an interesting offer arrived in my inbox. The poet laureate of Hawaii was coming to San Francisco to perform an evening-length epic poem and needed two dancers for the show. Did I know anyone who could choreograph and perform a five-minute duet depicting a celestial romance between the Earth and the moon?

Is age an issue? I emailed back. I didn't want to say Matt and I were north of forty.

The response, in words I had never heard in the ballet world, was *Why would it be?*

"Absolutely not," Matt said. "We don't look like dancers anymore. We look like old people."

I didn't tell him I had already accepted the gig or that I was hoping it would bring me some closure around ballet. Instead, I said, "Let's just go into the studio and see what we can do."

There would be no helicopter for the poet laureate. No tights and tutus either. We would wear casual clothes, abstractions for the celestial beings we represented. Rehearsals took place outside of work, sandwiched between ballet lessons and soccer practices. In one dance studio, we set up our kids with an iPad and a tub of LEGOs. In another, we choreographed in five-minute increments between interruptions. We worked quickly together, the way we did when we'd get three kids ready for school. What would have been five pirouettes a decade earlier was now a gentle pivot, a turn that slid into a roll. We replaced the helicopter and the fish with a simple overhead lift. Not flashy, but it fit.

Then the next day—panic. What if this performance wasn't enough? Dancing in Reykjavik hadn't been enough. Italy and San Francisco hadn't been enough. The castles, the Dying Swan solos, all the times I'd been a flower, a snowflake, Fritz—none of it had been enough. How could I be so naive to think that one more flit onstage would satisfy me?

On opening night, Matt and I applied our makeup in our shared dressing room. We reminisced about our careers. King City. Mountain View. The time we danced on a stage so small he had to shuffle backward during the lifts. The time we brought twin Pack 'n Plays to the theater to avoid paying for a babysitter.

We stood in the wings on opposite sides of the stage, and I was surprised that I could feel his resonance from so far away. It was the same connection I'd felt when we'd danced together before, but it was also the same harmony I'd felt in the panic of the NICU when the future was too scary to think about. The only thing we could grasp with any certainty was the present moment.

We took our places onstage as the music swirled around us, and I felt the familiar surge of adrenaline that only happened under stage lights in front of an audience. The feeling of tapping into a primordial energy that moved your limbs. The vibration of music that made your muscles sing.

When it was time for our overhead lift, I ran toward Matt on a sharp diagonal, but I overshot my plié. He hoisted me as if bench-pressing dead weight. This lift was supposed to be the shining jewel in our pas de deux, but I flubbed it. What should have been an arabesque high overhead, the way we'd planned, slid into an improvised pose that tipped and dipped before devolving into some other shape.

Instead of the tidal wave at the apex of our duet, it was seafoam dissolving into the rest of the dance.

Matt was characteristically sanguine about the mishap. "The audience was none the wiser," he pointed out. "No one knew we were going to do an overhead lift, anyway. And it's always fun just to do a show."

I disagreed. I didn't dance for funsies.

The year I danced for Michael Smuin, I was cast in a pas de deux set to the Beatles' "And I Love Her." I'd seen this ballet as a thirteen-year-old the summer I'd gone to San Francisco. Watching the ballet, I'd vowed to myself that one day I would dance for this Michael Smuin person, and I would dance this pas de deux. (You'd think that it would have been enough for me that my teen dream had come true, but of course, it wasn't.)

The costume was simple: a white long-sleeved leotard with a full-length white wraparound skirt that was so long in the back it dragged on the floor like a train of a wedding dress. Holding the hem of the skirt in my hand, the shape looked almost like a half-moon. Dancing with the skirt was similar to dancing in a Mexican folklórico dress minus the ruffles.

It also made dancing tricky. One night in performance, I skidded on the long train and smacked my face on the stage. I wasn't hurt, but it wasn't elegant, and there was no way to pretend that the slip was part of the choreography. I was mortified.

After the show, long after the audience had gone home, I stayed behind to rehearse myself. Repeating the steps responsible for the slip, I coordinated the swish of the skirt with the piqués of my pointe shoes. When I didn't execute the steps perfectly, I repeated the sequence. When I did execute the steps perfectly, I repeated the sequence. I stayed onstage for forty-five minutes and only left because the stagehands kicked me out.

To the outside eye, it looked like I was rehearsing my steps to prevent the fall from happening again, but really, it was a self-inflicted penance for the fact that it happened in the first place.

After the botched overhead lift for the poet laureate, I was similarly angry. Perhaps this impulse to punish myself was what led me to ballet class.

The class was called Ballet and Beats. I assumed this was an English translation of the French terms battu or batterie, which would mean the class involved more petite allegro than normal. Instead, it was a reference to the music—'80s radio hits instead of pianoforte. Depeche Mode. U2. Pet Shop Boys.

It's an entire playlist of my teen angst.

The very first plié transports me back in time. I am not a middle-aged woman in ballet flats and a leotard older than her firstborn child; I am sixteen again in a body that buzzes with desire but is reined in by the frustration of insecurity and self-loathing. My pores secrete a perspiration of raw emotions as I break into a sweat both real and metaphorical.

We do tendus to Prince and rond de jambe to the Police. Frappé to Men at Work. Grand battement to "Come On, Eileen."

When I was sixteen, every morning I woke up to an "ocean of never." I'd never lose those ten pounds. I'd never do a double pirouette en pointe. I'd never have an arabesque as high as the girls around me. I'd never fall in love or have a boyfriend. I'd never get a job. I'd never get noticed in the ballet studio.

The wounds are just as raw and fresh now as they were thirty years ago. The irony is not lost on me—aside from falling in love, my teenage list of aspirations has arced back to the unattainable. I will never again do a double pirouette en pointe or have an arabesque as high as the dancers around me.

But somewhere between A-ha's "Take on Me" and Journey's "Don't Stop Believin'," my heart cracks open, and I feel a flood of emotions without the self-recrimination. My mind has been calling this a "search," but my body intuits it is an ongoing excavation, digging through the day to let the light shine through.

So what if I don't get noticed in the ballet studio? It isn't about being seen. It's about showing yourself. After all, if the sun shines in the forest and there is no one to see it, it still shines.

We line up at the corner to waltz to Eurythmics' "Sweet Dreams (Are Made of This)." My limbs are liquid. I am floating. I am gliding. I am dancing. This is what it feels like to dance like a pretty girl, which my heart has always known, even if my head is just realizing it now.

FINALE

WE END UP IN THE AUDIENCE. I SUPPOSE I SHOULD HAVE SEEN this coming. I wear my most comfortable heels—the ones with the built-in arch supports—and my favorite KN95 mask, the one that doesn't pull off my earrings. I am glowing from the inside out.

I clutch my phone because it is both my ticket and my program, and Matt and I move at a snail's pace toward tonight's seats. The lobby bursts with patrons. San Francisco's old money is adorned in tennis bracelets, while the new money wears vegan leather and tennis shoes. There are little girls in frilly dresses and ballet students with their hair pulled taut into buns and couples who look just like us. There's a bottleneck at the entrance as the black pantsuit at the door examines each screen to verify vaccination status.

We find our row and seats, and I sit on the edge of mine. I'm just too excited to sit all the way back. After ninety years of existence, San Francisco Ballet has a woman as its director. Tonight we will see premiere works from two female choreographers. One is a woman of color. No more princesses and fairy tales. On the other side of the curtain, dancers are in various stages of stretching and smoking and praying. They are younger than I am and all better than I ever was. I can't wait to see them dance.

The curtain rises. Harps, strings, and horns coax and plead. The dancers answer with their bodies. My heart flutters and my muscles twitch with the vicarious thrill of dancing.

When one of the principal dancers melts into an arabesque that folds into multiple pirouettes, I gasp. The music is like taffy, and I can almost see the vibrations of sound reverberating off her, as if she can pull time and space, as if she can crawl in and out of the music and create something that almost isn't even seen; it's felt. For if it were only seen, every perfectly square arabesque would be just as exquisite as the next, when in fact, each one has its own moan, its own aria of beauty.

While I watch the dancers, my heart swells the same way it does when I watch my kids. Like the day I gave Chiara her first taste of ice cream. Or when John made Stonehenge out of tater tots on his highchair tray. Holding Wayne in the NICU when he grasped my thumb in his tiny hand. My heart even bursts for my younger self—the one who desperately wanted to be in "Waltz of the Flowers" and couldn't figure out how to dance like a pretty girl.

Again I am reminded: This is enough. All of it. To be here, to bear witness to what the human body can do. It is truly splendid and wondrous. In my home, in my heart. I just needed the right eyes to see it.

I squeeze Matt's hand, and he squeezes back.

CLARA WAKES FROM HER DREAM

TWO MONTHS BEFORE HER NINETY-EIGHTH BIRTHDAY, MS. Heuser came to me in a dream. I knew she was living in a memory care facility in El Paso. Over the years, her dancers would come to sit with her, finally letting go of their grudges.

Not I. I couldn't take the chance that after all these years, she would still take one final jab at me. Tell me that motherhood had made me fat or worse—drab. The most terrifying thought of all was that I'd visit and she'd pretend she didn't recognize me at all. Now she didn't remember anyone. It was too late.

In my dream, she had put together a version of *Swan Lake* in the backyard of a wealthy patron in San Francisco. It was a party scene with speaking roles. She was holding court.

"I'm French, you know," she said to the rest of the table, posing as she had in the "Prussian countess" photograph from my first Ballet El Paso program.

When it was my turn to speak, I turned to her and said, "Everything I know about manners I learned from you and Gigi."

She said that last part of the line with me, and I scowled. It was just like her to steal my thunder.

The swans never made it to the party.

Instead, each guest went in front of the audience to say what role they had been forced to play and who they really were inside. Sofia was there, along with my other friends from childhood. Some were dancers who'd gone on to dance in New York, San Francisco, and Sweden. Others had become teachers, lawyers, psychologists, or beauty queens.

While one of the dancers talked about his family, a storm hit a tree, spreading branches and splinters everywhere. Ms. Heuser ran to the man and his family, trying to remove the splinters. I panicked. I wanted very badly for the audience to know it wasn't real. We weren't really hurt. But her acting was so convincing. How would the audience see the difference between theater and life?

Lightning struck then and the performance stopped. The audience members dispersed, and I walked downtown through San Francisco to my home in Oakland.

Well, my dream-self thought, *there's another one of her shows that didn't work out.* Followed by *This drink is delicious. I think there are raisins in it.*

When I woke up, one hand was clasping the other.

I texted Sofia immediately.

Very vivid dream in the wee hours. I think Ms. Heuser is reaching out to us through our dreams to say she loves us and she's sorry.

She responded right away.

Ah! I believe that is true. How beautiful. Hang on to all that she taught us and give thanks for the world she created.

A few days later—on Valentine's Day—Sofia texted me.

Ms. Heuser passed away today. She was visiting you.

On Facebook, the tributes poured in. One dancer told of perpetually arriving late to class and being scolded. But her punctuality came at a cost: she came to class on an empty stomach. Ms. Heuser found out and, for the rest of the year, brought a sandwich for her young student to eat before class.

Memories surfaced, such as the time Ms. Heuser drove a handful of her favored students three hours north of El Paso to a ski resort in Ruidoso. We didn't ski, of course. That would have been too dangerous for our knees and ankles. Instead, we stomped around in the snow. To keep our feet dry, Ms. Heuser handed out bread bags to wear over our shoes, fastening the plastic around our shins with string. For over an hour, Dee Bee, Sofia, and I happily trudged up one of the bunny slopes close to the parking lot with the rest of our class, staying on the sidelines away from the real skiers, as if we were dancing in the wings. We shrieked as we inched down the hill in our makeshift snow gear. The day was sunny. The snow was sloshy.

People remembered other odd kindnesses, such as when Ms. Heuser returned from her annual visit to Germany bearing gifts: leotards, pointe shoes, and hair pins smuggled out of the opera company of her youth.

I don't remember gifts from Germany, but I do remember the year I lost all my friends in Mrs. Vogel's class, the year of my first *Nutcracker*. I was twelve. By this time, I knew how to dress like a professional student. I knew what brand of black leotard to wear and how to pull up my tights so they didn't bag at the knees. I worked up the nerve to ask if I could choreograph a dance for the spring recital. Ms. Heuser didn't say yes right away. She gave me a list of conditions and a timeline of two weeks.

Two weeks later I showed her the dance I'd created.

When I finished, she said nothing. Instead, she took me by the hand and led me to the stereo. We listened to the music I'd chosen. Once, twice, three times.

Finally she spoke. "A dance is a story," she said. "Even when it doesn't have a storyline. Do you hear this opening melody?" She paused. "Here it is again! But a little different this time."

And then she told me my dance was very good. "But here's how to make it better."

There was another rehearsal scheduled, but Ms. Heuser didn't start it right away. Instead, holding my hand, we went through all the patterns of my choreography, where the steps could progress, how a step could be reminiscent of another one without being repetitive. At the end of our hour, she asked who I would cast in my ballet, and I told her. I picked three dancers from the class below mine. She nodded her approval.

She must have let me perform the dance in the recital—I would have carried a grudge if she hadn't. But I have no recollection of the performance. What I remember is the tenderness, not just with me but with the idea of dance itself. As if each tendu, each glissade, were a precious object to be venerated, arranged with the same delicate care one would use with any exquisite piece of art: a priceless painting or a diamond necklace. She taught me that choreography can be beautiful even before there is a dancer to execute it.

Two days before she died, Ms. Heuser came to me in another dream. We were at Magoffin Auditorium, the theater at the university. She sat in the audience dressed as the Queen of England, complete with tiara, white gloves, and a ruby-encrusted scepter.

Kendal was there, one of the dancers Ms. Heuser fired when I was in middle school, along with all the dancers hired in the intervening years because they looked like Kendal.

I was onstage with Sofia and all the Kendals dancing "Mother Ginger," but as an adult. None of us could see anything. The theater was so much darker than in a real performance. There were no stage lights, no house lights. Not even the ghost light shone.

We could only hear the sound of her voice.

You are beautiful.

ACKNOWLEDGMENTS

One of the marks of an excellent performance is the appearance of effortlessness that leaves the audience completely unaware of how many cast and crew have contributed to the production from behind the scenes. Without them, there is no show.

And so it is with a book.

The curtain that closed briefly after the last line draws open again. I jump to my feet, applauding and cheering for my metaphorical stagehands and costume designers, without whom this book would just be a shoebox of postcards, Post-it notes, and journal entries.

First, from opposite sides of the stage, the writing groups join hands and run to the center. They are Kate Hopper and the Fisher Cats, the Unicorn Author Club, the Slug Sisters of Hedgebrook, and the Flying Flounders of Zoom, followed by the Cabana Boys of Vashon Island, who sport clown masks and orca costumes as they throw popcorn at the audience.

Then the cheerleaders bow, starting with my Moon Circle Goddesses—Sweta, Susan, Sheree, and Katie—fearless women who inspire me with their strength and grace. On their heels are the Cousin-O-Ramans and Selected Wannabes, who are also fearless, but with fewer chants and more cheeseballs.

There are the friends and role models whose artistry made me a better dancer: Renée Fairweather, Sofia Larkin, DB Lampman, Amy London, David Duran, Mika Vinson, Francia Russell, Alan Howard, Elroy Bode, Robert North, and, of course, Ingeborg Heuser, who curtsies the way the Russians do, with two counts for each gesture. Roses drop from the balcony.

Next we see the literary journals who published early chapters of this book, Layne Mandros and the team from Books Forward, and the crew from She Writes Press whose hard work made me a better writer and made this a better book—Brooke Warner, Lauren Wise, Julie Metz, MaryAnn Smith, and Stacey Aaronson. They hold hands and bow together.

A round of applause for my early readers: Jackie Bryan, Marianne Lonsdale, Sara Nović, Toni Mirosevich, Putsata Reang, Naomi Williams, Jessica Rae Bergamino, Andrea Torres, Harriet Heydemann, Savala Nolan, Saskia Kovac, Laurie Cunningham, Tanya Warren, and Fulvio Faudella. *Bravi!*

Voices from the dress circle cheer for the writing spaces: Willow Cottage and the Meadow House at Hedgebrook, the Mesa Refuge, In Cahoots, the Oakland Peace Center, and the chalkboards of the Mineral School. Leo and the rest of the ghosts in Veltin Studio at MacDowell. The always generous Naomi Goldner and Tom Phillips, whose WordSpace Studios was invaluable during final edits.

Lorriane Fico-White, who requested those final edits and whose exploration of present tense paved the way for a gratifying journey into the past, gets her own curtain call.

As does Sam Kasprowicz for her ode to Degas and her beautiful silhouette of young dancer Maria von Goethem.

Our hands buzz from the applause, but we're not done yet.

Soloists take their bows in a center spotlight:

Tarja Parssinen, who said, "*That's* your universal theme."

Jessica O'Dwyer, who said, "*That's* your title."

Rachel Sarah, who said, "*That's* your *Nutcracker* book."

Minal Hajratwala, who said, "Everything you need is already here."

The stage is almost completely full, and we know that the

final performers are those who, by their unwavering love and support, truly made this show worthy of its encore.

My parents, Jerry and Marian. My siblings, Jason, Jeff, Jackie, and Liz. My beautiful kids, Chiara, Michael, and Wagner. You are my first-cast heroes.

My mother, Phoebe, who in the beginning drove to every rehearsal and paid for all the pointe shoes and now reads every line and makes every comma earn its keep.

Thank you.

And finally, for Matt, the best partner I've ever had. May we never work this hard for a unitard ever again.

ABOUT THE AUTHOR

JANINE KOVAC enjoyed a twelve-year career as a professional ballet dancer in Iceland, Italy, San Francisco, and her hometown of El Paso, Texas. Outside of the ballet world, her distinctions include UC Berkeley's Glushko Award for Distinguished Research in Cognitive Science, an Elizabeth George Foundation Fellowship from Hedgebrook, and the Calderwood Fellowship for Journalism from MacDowell. Janine is the author of *Brain Changer: A Mother's Guide to Cognitive Science* and *Spinning: Choreography for Coming Home,* which received a National Indie Excellence Award. In addition to dancing in *The Nutcracker,* she's rehearsed *The Nutcracker,* she's choreographed sections of *The Nutcracker,* and, most of all, she's sat through *The Nutcracker.* Janine lives with her family in Oakland, California.

Looking for your next great read?

We can help!

Visit www.shewritespress.com/next-read
or scan the QR code below for a list
of our recommended titles.

She Writes Press is an award-winning
independent publishing company founded to
serve women writers everywhere.